149

To the Yalu

FROM THE CHINESE INVASION OF KOREA TO MACARTHUR'S DISMISSAL

To the Yalu

FROM THE CHINESE INVASION OF KOREA TO MACARTHUR'S DISMISSAL

by James McGovern

William Morrow & Company, Inc.

 New York 1972

Photo credits: U. S. Army

For my daughter, Lisa McGovern

Contents

Illustrations between pages 106 and 107

Chronology of Major Events

Dating the major events described in this book is complicated by the fact that Korea and the United States are separated by the International Date Line. Korean time, for example, was fourteen hours in advance of eastern daylight time in Washington when North Korea attacked South Korea. I have therefore used Korean time (KT) for events taking place in that country and elsewhere in the Far East and Washington time (WT) for events in Washington and at the United Nations in Lake Success, New York.

DATE   EVENT

1950
June
25 KT   North Korea invades South Korea.

25 WT   The U.S. Joint Chiefs of Staff authorize General MacArthur to use U.S. Air and Navy to evacuate Americans and deliver supplies to the South Korean Army.

DATE   EVENT

1950
June
26 WT   Joint Chiefs direct MacArthur to use U.S. Air
             and Navy to support South Korean Army south
             of 38th Parallel.

27 KT   South Korean capital of Seoul falls to Communists.

July
 8 WT   General MacArthur appointed commander of
             U.N. military forces.

September
15 KT   MacArthur directs landing at Inchon, which al-
             most destroys North Korean Army.

25 KT   Chinese Communists warn Indian ambassador in
             Peking of possible Chinese intervention.

27 WT   Joint Chiefs authorize MacArthur to take action
             north of the 38th Parallel, but limit action in
             provinces bordering on Manchuria to South Ko-
             rean troops.

28 KT   Seoul is liberated.

October
 1 KT   MacArthur demands North Korea surrender.

 1 KT   Chou En-lai speech warns of Chinese intervention.

 3 KT   Chou En-lai warns Indian ambassador in Peking
             of Chinese intervention.

 7 WT   General Assembly of United Nations passes reso-
             lution authorizing use of U.N. troops anywhere
             north of 38th Parallel to establish unified and
             democratic Korea.

 7 KT   U.S. troops cross 38th Parallel.

 9 KT   MacArthur again demands North Korean surren-
             der; no reply.

DATE   EVENT

1950
October
14 KT   Chinese troops begin crossing Yalu River.

15 KT   Wake Island meeting between Truman and Mac-
             Arthur.

19 KT   North Korean capital of Pyongyang captured by
             U.N.

24 KT   MacArthur orders U.S. as well as South Korean
             troops to drive to Yalu River border between
             China and North Korea; his action questioned by
             Joint Chiefs.

25 KT   South Korean battalion in far north attacked by
             Chinese troops.

November
 1 KT   U.S. units attacked by Chinese.

 1 KT   Soviet-built MIG jets cross Yalu.

2–3 KT   8th Army in northwest and U.S. 1st Marine Di-
             vision in northeast come under heavy Chinese
             attack.

 4 WT   Joint Chiefs receive message from MacArthur
             discounting seriousness of Chinese attacks.

 6 KT   Chinese begin to break off their attacks.

 7 KT   MacArthur denied authorization for hot pursuit
             of MIG jets into Manchuria.

 6 KT   MacArthur makes public complaint about Chi-
             nese Communist forces crossing the Yalu, but no
             new directive sent to him by Washington to halt
             advance north.

21 KT   U.S. 17th Regimental Combat Team reaches
             Yalu.

DATE   EVENT

1950
November

24 KT   8th Army begins major offensive; MacArthur announces that, if successful, it will end war.

26 KT   Chinese counterattack in force.

28 KT   MacArthur communiqué announces he is faced with "new war." U.N. forces begin retreat.

30 WT   Truman makes comment about use of atom bomb at press conference.

30 KT   MacArthur begins series of public complaints about limitations on his command.

December

3 KT   8th Army escapes entrapment but continues retreat south.

3 WT   Joint Chiefs inform MacArthur that his mission is now to consolidate his forces on beachheads.

4 WT   Prime Minister Attlee arrives in Washington.

5 KT   Pyongyang abandoned by U.N.

11 KT   1st Marine Division reaches safety at northeast evacuation port of Hamhung-Hungnam. Chinese begin to break off attacks.

14 WT   United Nations passes resolution seeking cease-fire.

16 WT   Truman announces national emergency.

22 WT   Chinese Communists reject cease-fire.

31 KT   New Chinese offensive begins.

1951
January

4 KT   Seoul abandoned.

9 KT   MacArthur receives negative reply from Joint Chiefs on his recommendations for strong retali-

DATE   EVENT

1951
January

atory measures against Chinese. The General be-
comes increasingly resentful of restrictions.

14 KT   MacArthur receives placating cable from Truman.

20 KT   MacArthur visits front in Korea and displays renewed confidence. Fighting begins to become
stalemated around 38th Parallel.

February
 1 WT   United Nations condemns Communist China as
aggressor. Inconclusive fighting continues.

March
 7 KT   MacArthur makes public protest to war correspondents about military restrictions.

20 WT   MacArthur informed that presidential announcement is forthcoming about seeking peace in
Korea.

24 KT   MacArthur issues his own announcement.

April
 5 WT   Representative Martin reads MacArthur's reply
to his letter of March 8.

11 KT   MacArthur receives news of his relief by President Truman.

May
 3 WT   MacArthur hearings begin.

July
10 KT   Truce talks start in Korea, but indecisive fighting
continues.

1953
July
27 KT   Armistice signed.

Author to Reader

The first American ship to reach China landed at Canton on August 30, 1784. The ship carried an export cargo of ginseng, a rare herb prized by Chinese physicians as a prolonger of life and an aphrodisiac. The arrival of the *Empress of China,* as the vessel was named, began United States relations with China.

In 1811, the first of an ever-growing number of Christian missionaries went to China. Thirty-three years later the first treaty between China and the United States gave America the same "extraterritorial" rights that European nations had previously gained. Further relations were marked by ties of friendship, trade, philanthropy, education, missionary activity, and support of the Chiang Kai-shek regime in the war against Japan from 1937 to 1945. These ties came to an end in 1949 when the Communists gained control of mainland China.

After Japan surrendered in 1945, President Truman ordered U.S. forces to help more than six hundred thousand Chinese Nationalist soldiers move into north and central China to prevent a Communist takeover. But despite two billion dollars in aid and the full pressure of American political influence, the

United States could not sustain the Chiang Kai-shek regime in its civil war with the Communists. The Nationalist Chinese, plagued by inflation, corruption, internal dissension, and a mood of hopelessness, disintegrated and fled to the offshore island of Formosa (Taiwan) in 1949.

The Truman Administration, with the backing of the Republican opposition, continued to support the Nationalist Chinese on Taiwan. But Truman did discourage Chiang Kai-shek from attempting to invade the mainland. In turn, the President directed the U.S. Seventh Fleet to prevent the Communists from invading Taiwan. This directive incensed Peking, which saw it as another Western intrusion into Chinese affairs and did not believe there could be "two Chinas."

During this entire period of America's involvement with China, Korea did not play much of a role in the American consciousness. And yet Korea shared a common border with Chinese Manchuria and had strong ties to China. Korea adopted its literature and writing system, but not its language, from China, as well as the Buddhist religion and Confucian social system and governmental forms and institutions. However, Korea was known as the "Hermit Kingdom" because of the strict isolationism it practiced as protection against its powerful neighbors, Japan and China. Korea did not fall under foreign political domination in modern times until its annexation as a colony by Japan in 1910.

After the defeat of Japan in 1945, Korea was divided, at the 38th Parallel, into the Soviet Russian (North Korean) and United States (South Korean) zones of occupation. The Russians came down from Manchuria, from which they had recently ejected the Japanese.

In 1948, rival governments were established in the industrial north of 9 million people and the agricultural south of 21 million people. Relations between them became strained after the departure of Russian and American occupation forces. Early on the morning of June 25, 1950, forces of the Democratic People's Republic of Korea, skillfully employing Russian tanks, struck south at the Republic of Korea.

The South Korean soldiers fell back, often abandoning their American equipment in panic. The United States Joint Chiefs of Staff, realizing that the South Koreans would soon be overwhelmed if not given assistance, directed General of the Army Douglas MacArthur on June 26 to provide them with American naval and air support south of the 38th Parallel. At this time, no one in the United States Government appeared to have given any thought to the possibility that Communist China might have a stake in what happened to its smaller neighbor.

In Tokyo, MacArthur was then, as Supreme Commander for Allied Powers, directing the occupation of Japan. He had no responsibility whatever for Korea. The country had been declared to be outside the Far Eastern defense perimeter of the United States by Secretary of State Dean Acheson on January 12, 1950. Since MacArthur was also Commander-in-chief, Far East, and as such commander of all United States Army, Navy, and Air Forces in that area, he was the logical choice of the Joint Chiefs for the direction of military support for the South Koreans.

On June 29, 1950, as the South Koreans continued to be driven back, the Joint Chiefs of Staff authorized MacArthur to use American ground troops in South Korea and to take air and naval action north of the 38th Parallel. At this time, no authorization was given to employ American ground troops in North Korea.

The United Nations authorized its member nations to give military support to South Korea and on July 7 requested the United States to appoint a commander for the unified United Nations forces. The next day, President Truman announced the appointment of General MacArthur as the U.N. Commander.

Until the end of August 1950, when the first British Commonwealth ground troops arrived, only air and naval elements were provided by U.N. member nations other than the United States. But by the end of 1951, fifteen U.N. members had contributed armed forces to assist the South Korean Army: Australia, Belgium, Canada, Colombia, Ethiopia, France,

Greece, Netherlands, New Zealand, Philippines, South Africa, Thailand, Turkey, the United States, and the United Kingdom. These forces, apart from those of the United States, were of a token, symbolic nature. As of September 30, 1950, the United Nations Command ground strength consisted of 113,494 Americans and 104,048 South Koreans, with the next largest number of ground combat forces being those from Great Britain, 1704, and the Philippines, 1369.

By the end of August 1950, South Korean and American troops had been forced to retreat to the Pusan area at the southeast tip of Korea. They held there and began a counter-offensive after a landing was made on September 15 at Inchon on the west coast. The North Korean People's Army began to retreat deep into North Korea, and General MacArthur demanded its surrender on October 1. He received no reply.

MacArthur was ready to finish off the North Koreans above the 38th Parallel with a coordinated ground-sea-air offensive and on October 9 broadcast a second ultimatum: "I, as the United Nations Commander-in-Chief, for the last time call upon you and the forces under your command, in whatever part of Korea situated, forthwith to lay down your arms and cease hostilities."

Again, there was no reply. Then, on October 12, President Truman requested General MacArthur to meet him somewhere in the Pacific. "I knew nothing of the purpose of the meeting," the General wrote in his *Reminiscences,* "my only information being that Averell Harriman would be there."

In his announcement to the American public, who believed that the conflict in Korea was almost over, President Truman offered no specific or urgent reasons for calling this meeting. "General MacArthur and I," the public announcement stated in part, "are making a quick trip over the coming weekend to meet in the Pacific. . . . I shall discuss with him the final phase of United Nations action in Korea. . . . [and] . . . other matters within his responsibility."

A few minutes after midnight on Saturday, October 14, President Truman left Hickam Field, Hawaii, on the final, twenty-three-hundred-mile leg of his flight to a remote island in the Pacific. There he would indeed discuss with MacArthur the "final phase of United Nations action in Korea." Instead of being an end, however, the conference would really mark the beginning of a series of events that would result in one of history's greatest examples of human fallibility, bring the United Nations Command to the brink of destruction, and poise the world on the edge of a general war in which the opposing sides both possessed nuclear weapons.

To the Yalu

FROM THE CHINESE INVASION OF KOREA
TO MacARTHUR'S DISMISSAL

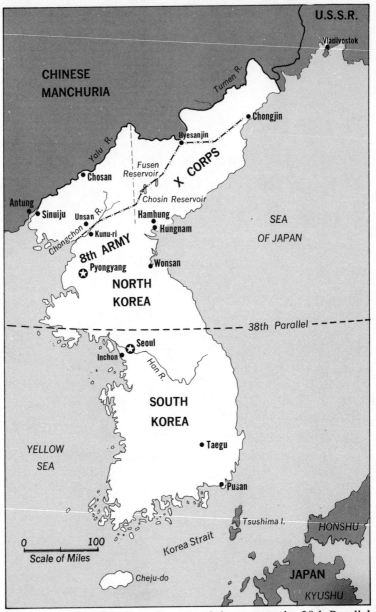

General MacArthur's U.N. Command drove over the 38th Parallel into North Korea on October 1, 1950. By November 24, the divided command (8th Army on the left, X Corps on the right) had reached the line shown by the dotted line and launched an offensive to "end the war." The Chinese counterattacked two days later and drove the U.N. Command seventy miles below the 38th Parallel by January 22, 1951.

CHAPTER
ONE

Wake Island

A great black thundercloud drifted in the east as President Truman's DC-6, the *Independence,* began to circle Wake Island in the dim early light of Sunday, October 15, 1950. After a seven-thousand-mile flight that had brought him two-thirds of the way around the world the President was nearing a square-mile dot of scrub-covered sand and coral midway between Japan and Hawaii. Wake Island's entire military garrison normally consisted of six U.S. coast guardsmen engaged in setting up a navigation system. But on this particular morning, General of the Army Douglas MacArthur was waiting for Mr. Truman on the island's airplane runway.

MacArthur had spent the night on Wake Island, having flown in twelve hours earlier from Tokyo. In that city, seventeen hundred miles away, he was Supreme Commander for Allied Powers and as such the real ruler of 83 million Japanese. For the past four months, he had also commanded United Nations military forces in Korea.

Since victory for the United Nations now seemed to depend on mopping up what was left of the North Korean armed forces, the General asked himself why the President thought it

1

necessary to request this meeting. However, Brigadier General Courtney Whitney detected a motive for Truman's unique trip. Whitney was MacArthur's chief political confidant in Tokyo and had accompanied him to Wake Island. Congressional elections were only two weeks away in the United States. Whitney suspected that the President might be trying to gain favor with the voters by establishing a closer connection between his administration and the victorious General.

The *Independence* landed, taxied past the rusting hulks of World War II Japanese tanks and the General's personal plane —a new silver Constellation named *SCAP,* for Supreme Commander for Allied Powers—and rolled to a halt. Truman emerged from the *Independence* to see MacArthur waiting for him at the foot of the landing ramp. The General wore ordinary suntan khakis, without decorations, in the Pacific heat. However, his open collar bore the five small stars of a General of the Army and he wore a gilt-encrusted cap that struck the President as having "evidently seen a good deal of use."

Truman knew that there was widespread speculation about his motives for calling this midocean meeting. But he felt that he had at least two good reasons for doing so. The first was that he had never met MacArthur and wanted, in person, to make certain that the General was in agreement with the worldwide aims of the Administration's foreign policy. This was principally designed to contain Soviet Russia in Europe and secondarily to contain communism in the Far East. MacArthur had served continuously in the Far East for thirteen years, and the President felt that all of the General's thoughts were "wrapped up" there.

In seeing MacArthur for the first time, Truman was looking at a man who aroused strong reactions. In the judgment of Field Marshal Alanbrooke, Chief of the British Imperial General Staff in World War II, MacArthur was "the greatest general and the best strategist that the war produced." Winston Churchill described him as the outstanding general of the war that had ended five years before. Arthur Hays Sulzberger, publisher of *The New York Times,* and that newspaper's newly appointed assistant managing editor, Turner Catledge, had been briefed by MacArthur in November 1944 at Leyte in the Philippines on his plans to recapture the rest of those islands from the Japanese. "As he spoke," Catledge later wrote, "he was variously the military expert, the political figure, the man of destiny. . . . Sulzberger and I later agreed that we had never met a more egotistical man, nor one more aware of his egotism and more able and determined to back it up with his deeds."

In meeting Truman, the General did not salute his Commander-in-chief. Instead, MacArthur pumped the President's right hand in a warm, genial manner, holding Truman's right elbow with his other hand while doing so.

The President grinned and said: "How are you, General? I've been a long time meeting you, General."

"I hope it won't be so long next time," MacArthur answered.

After some thirty-five photographers from two planes that had accompanied the *Independence* finished what the President characterized as "their usual picture orgy," Truman and MacArthur walked arm in arm to a dusty, black 1948 Chevrolet sedan, the best transportation the island could provide. The President motioned the General to enter the car first as aides attached presidential flags to its front fenders.

The two men were then driven to a Quonset hut just off the airstrip, which normally served as the office of the island manager for Pan American Airways. Once inside the office Truman sat down on a wicker chair, MacArthur on a rattan settee. The door was closed. This was to be a private meeting, from which admirals, generals, ambassadors, and the press were barred.

The conversation was very friendly, much more so than the President had expected, and the two men seemed to like each other. Truman found the General to be "a most stimulating and interesting person," while MacArthur felt that the President radiated courtesy and good humor. The cordiality must have pleasantly surprised the General who, as he later wrote, "had been warned about Mr. Truman's quick and violent temper and prejudices."

In addition to meeting MacArthur, the President's other primary reason for making this trip was to get the benefit of the General's "firsthand information and judgment concerning China." While the North Korean invasion of South Korea had been repulsed and the North Korean Army almost destroyed by MacArthur's tactics, the Chinese had cast a somewhat mystifying shadow over an otherwise bright picture.

North Korea bordered on Chinese Manchuria for 580 miles and for 25 miles in its northeast corner on Russian Siberia. The Chinese Communist Government had only been in power for a year in Peking since defeating the Nationalists in their civil war. Now Peking was threatening to act if the United Nations Command crossed the 38th Parallel into North Korea and approached the Chinese border, over a third of which followed the Yalu River.

As early as July, the Joint Chiefs of Staff in Washington had received "brief intimations," according to J. Lawton Collins, Army Chief of Staff, that the Chinese Communists were moving their troops toward the Manchurian side of the common border with North Korea and might enter the conflict. President Truman certainly did not want to risk allowing this limited war in Korea to expand into a land war of attrition with China, whose 600 million people made it the most populous nation on earth. MacArthur's opinion about the possibility of Chinese intervention would be extremely valuable. He was regarded as an expert on Oriental affairs and 90 percent of intelligence on the Far East came to Washington from his command.

During their private talk, according to Truman, MacArthur told the President that the Chinese Communists would not attack and that victory was won. The General never commented on this private talk. When it ended, after about an hour, the two men emerged from the Quonset hut into the tropic sunshine and were driven to Wake Island's new coral-

pink Administration Building for a second conference, to
which their advisers were admitted. The President, removing
his coat, sat down at the head of a long table. MacArthur,
producing a long-stemmed briar pipe, asked: "Do you mind if
I smoke, Mr. President?"

"No," said Truman, a nonsmoker. "I suppose I've had more
smoke blown in my face than any other man alive." This reply
was greeted by laughter, which MacArthur thought Truman
seemed to enjoy.

The eight members of the President's party who sat around
the table included General Omar Bradley, Chairman of the
Joint Chiefs of Staff; Dean Rusk, who was in charge of Far
Eastern Affairs for the State Department; and Special Adviser
Averell Harriman, who was Ambassador to the Soviet Union
during World War II.

Noting that Colonel Laurence Bunker, aide-de-camp to
MacArthur, was preparing to take notes, Truman's Press Secretary, Charlie Ross, told the General that no record of this
conference was to be made. However, Vernice Anderson,
secretary to United Nations Ambassador Philip Jessup, was
sitting next door. Although no one told her to do so, she began
to take down stenographic notes.

To MacArthur, this second conference was "innocuous
enough" and its "sketchy agenda" contained nothing upon
which his fullest views had not already been made known to
the Administration. He answered many questions dealing with
such problems as Korea's postwar rehabilitation and the
Japanese peace treaty. The President was impressed by the
General's firm statement that the Korean War would be over
by Thanksgiving and that it might be possible to withdraw all
non-Korean troops from the country by January 1951.

As the conference neared its end, Truman brought up a
subject that he had discussed with MacArthur in their earlier
private conference, that of Chinese intervention. On October
1, MacArthur had sent South Korean troops over the 38th
Parallel into North Korea. The President knew that on
October 3 the Chinese Premier and Foreign Minister, Chou

En-lai, had summoned the Indian Ambassador to China, Sirdar K. M. Panikkar, to Chou's official residence in Peking. Chou told Panikkar that China would enter the war if the Americans also crossed the parallel. "The South Koreans did not matter," Chou said, "but American intrusion into North Korea would encounter Chinese resistance."

Chou's warning could not be addressed officially to either the United Nations or to President Truman because Peking had no seat in the U.N. and the United States declined to maintain diplomatic relations with Communist China. And so, ignoring Chou's warning, Truman had allowed MacArthur to send American troops across the parallel on October 7. In doing so, the President had the sanction of the United Nations.

The original purpose of the United Nations intervention in June was "solely for the purpose of restoring the Republic of Korea to its status prior to the invasion of the north." * But on October 7 the General Assembly had passed a resolution authorizing the use of U.N. troops in any part of Korea in order to establish a "unified, independent and democratic government." This resolution, in effect, sanctioned an invasion of North Korea by the United Nations. It was passed by a vote of 47 to 5.

The five negative votes came from the Soviet bloc. Seven nations, including India, Yugoslavia, and part of the Arab bloc, abstained from voting. These seven nations, in particular India, felt that Russia and China might be provoked into entering the war by a United Nations move into North Korea. Peking, of course, could cast no vote on the issue.

The forty-seven nations, led by the United States, who voted for entering North Korea did so in the belief that the Chinese Communists did not mean what they were saying through unofficial channels. With the collapse of the North Korean Army, the opportunity to occupy all of North Korea and turn it into a democratic state appeared too tempting to be ignored.

Now, eight days after the passage of the U.N. resolution, the

* *State Department Bulletin,* XXIII (July 10, 1950), 579-80.

President asked the General: "What are the chances for Chinese or Soviet interference?"

"Very little," MacArthur replied, according to Miss Anderson's stenographic notes. "Had they interfered in the first or second months it would have been decisive. We are no longer fearful of their intervention. We no longer stand hat in hand. The Chinese have 300,000 men in Manchuria. Of these probably not more than 100/125,000 are distributed along the Yalu River. They have no air force. Now that we have our Air Force in Korea, if the Chinese tried to get down to Pyongyang [the North Korean capital] there would be the greatest slaughter."

The General also discounted Soviet intervention. He said that the Russians had no ground troops available for North Korea. While granting that the Soviet Air Force stationed in Siberia was a "fairly good one, with excellent pilots," he said that any attempt by the Russians to give air support to Chinese infantrymen would result in the Soviets bombing "the Chinese as often as they would bomb us."

Neither the President, nor any of his advisers, disputed MacArthur's opinion that there was "very little" chance of the Chinese or the Russians entering the Korean War. Averell Harriman then changed the subject by asking the General: "What about war criminals?"

"Don't touch the war criminals," MacArthur replied. "It doesn't work. The Nurnberg trials and the Tokyo trials were no deterrent. In my own right I can handle those who have committed atrocities and, if we catch them, I intend to try them immediately by military commission."

Shortly thereafter, the conference was concluded by President Truman with the statement: "The communiqué should be submitted as soon as it is ready and General MacArthur can return immediately. This has been a most satisfactory conference."

While waiting for the communiqué to be prepared, Truman and MacArthur engaged in small talk. The General asked the President if he would run for reelection in 1952. Instead of responding to this question, Truman asked MacArthur if he had any presidential ambitions. There had been small Republican booms for the General in 1944 and 1948. In the latter year he had received 11 out of a possible 1,094 votes at the Republican National Convention.

"None whatsoever," MacArthur replied. "If you have any general running against you, his name will be Eisenhower, not MacArthur."

Before boarding the *Independence* at the airstrip, Truman pinned a new Oak Leaf Cluster to the Distinguished Service Medal on MacArthur's open-necked shirt, the fifth time the General had been awarded this decoration.

Exuding enthusiasm, Truman told reporters that he'd never had a more satisfactory conference since he'd been President and referred to MacArthur as "one of America's greatest soldier-statesmen."

The General, frequently consulting his watch as though to be off to more pressing matters, said only: "All the comments will have to come from the publicity man for the President." However, MacArthur did authorize the President's Press Secretary to state: "No field commander in the history of warfare has had more complete and admirable support than I have during the Korean operation." Privately, the General had some strong doubts about the President's grasp of the situation. He thought that during both conferences Truman had displayed a superficial knowledge of history and little understanding of the Far East.

Twenty-five minutes before noon and five hours after arriving on Wake Island, Truman took off in the *Independence* for Hawaii to the cheers of two hundred Guamanian, Filipino, and Marshallese airfield laborers. Five minutes later, MacArthur departed in the *SCAP* for Tokyo. There he would resume his interrupted business of directing the United Nations offensive in the limited war that the General had told the President would be over by Thanksgiving.

CHAPTER
TWO

Warnings

Almost immediately after arriving on the mainland, the President spoke at the Opera House in San Francisco, where the United Nations had been founded five years earlier.

"I have just returned from Wake Island," he said, "where I had a most satisfactory conference with General Douglas MacArthur.

"I understand that there has been speculation about why I made this trip. There is really no mystery about it. I went because I wanted to see and talk to General MacArthur. The best way to see him and talk to him is to meet him somewhere and talk to him. . . . I also felt that there was pressing need to make it perfectly clear—by my talk with General Mac-Arthur—that there is complete unity in the aims and conduct of our foreign policy."

The President expressed his satisfaction with the results of the conference and his confidence that peace would soon be restored to all of Korea. He also called upon the Soviet Union to abandon its policy of Communist imperialism and to join the rest of the United Nations in calling upon the North Koreans to lay down their arms at once.

Nowhere in his lengthy public report, with its many references to the aggressive Russians, did the President mention the Communist Chinese threats to enter the Korean War. And yet, privately, Mr. Truman had good reason to be concerned about them.

Originally, the warnings could be dismissed as bluff or propaganda. But they became more pointed and hostile with the successful advance of MacArthur's command and the inability of the North Koreans to cope with it. On September 25, fifteen days before the Wake Island conference, Indian Ambassador Panikkar had an informal after-dinner conversation in Peking with General Nieh Jung-chen, Acting Chief of Staff of the People's Liberation Army. General Nieh told the ambassador that China would not "sit back with folded hands and let the Americans come to the border."

When Panikkar suggested that war with the United States could lead to great destruction for China and set her back by half a century, General Nieh laughed and said: "We have calculated all that. . . . They may even drop atom bombs on us. What then? They may kill a few million people. Without sacrifice, a nation's independence cannot be upheld. . . . After all, China lives on the farms. What can atom bombs do there?"

Seven days after this private conversation, the substance of which was passed on to Washington by the Indian government, Chou En-lai made a lengthy speech in Peking reporting on the results of the first year of Communist rule. In the course of this speech, Chou said: "The Chinese people absolutely will not tolerate foreign aggression, nor will they supinely tolerate seeing their neighbors being savagely invaded by imperialists."

On October 3 came Chou's warning to Panikkar that "American intrusion into North Korea would encounter Chinese resistance." And on October 10, five days before the Wake Island conference, the Chinese Ministry of Foreign Affairs issued this warning: "Now that the American forces are attempting to cross the 38th Parallel on a large scale, the

Chinese people cannot stand idly by with regard to such a serious situation created by the invasion of Korea. . . ."

These threats, along with many others, were considered but not taken literally in Washington. President Truman and his closest advisers tended to downgrade the reports of Indian Ambassador Panikkar as those of a gullible fellow traveler. "The problem that arose in connection with these reports," Truman later wrote, "was that Mr. Panikkar had in the past played the game of the Chinese Communists fairly regularly, so that his statement could not be taken as that of an impartial observer."

As for Chou En-lai's warning, the President categorized it as "a bald attempt to blackmail the United Nations." Communist China was not a member of the U.N. The United States opposed her admission and also declined to recognize Communist China diplomatically. This made communication between the two countries dependent on third parties.

Secretary of State Dean Acheson did not take the Chinese threats seriously either. Back on September 10, he had declared: "I think it would be sheer madness on the part of the Chinese Communists to do that [intervene] and I see no advantage to them in doing it." And at a press conference on October 4 at United Nations Headquarters in Lake Success, New York, Acheson maintained that "there was reason to believe that Communist China would not send troops into North Korea." It was a premise of his Far Eastern policy that there was greater likelihood of conflict between the long-term interests of China and the Soviet Union than between those of China and the United States.

On October 12, three days before the Wake Island conference, the Central Intelligence Agency reported to President Truman that Chinese entry into the Korean War was "not probable in 1950" because the Chinese feared the consequences of war with America. And then, at Wake Island itself, MacArthur had told the President that there was "very little" chance of the Chinese entering the war.

The Central Intelligence Agency and the Secretary of State

thus found themselves agreeing with General MacArthur and his Far East Command Military Intelligence in mid-October. None of them believed what the Chinese Communists were saying and advised the President to that effect. The result was that Truman, in accordance with the United Nations resolution of October 7, allowed MacArthur to drive ever deeper into North Korea.

The sanctioning of the northward drive was a political decision. From the military viewpoint, the Joint Chiefs of Staff remained concerned about the possibility of Chinese intervention. They did not instruct MacArthur to halt his drive or make it clear to the President that the General was engaged in a gamble. But the Joint Chiefs did at least forward to MacArthur directives designed to prevent American troops from coming to battle with the Chinese or Russians. On September 27, the Joint Chiefs informed the United Nations Commander that:

> Your military objective is the destruction of the North Korean armed forces. In attaining this objective you are authorized to conduct military operations . . . north of the 38th Parallel in Korea, provided that at the time of such operations there has been no entry into North Korea by major Soviet or Chinese Communist forces, no announcement of intended entry, nor a threat to counter our operations militarily in North Korea. Under no circumstances, however, will your forces cross the Manchurian or USSR borders of Korea and, as a matter of policy, no non-Korean ground forces will be used in the northeast provinces bordering the Soviet Union or in the area along the Manchurian border.

However, on September 30 in Tokyo, MacArthur received a personal letter from Secretary of Defense George C. Marshall, which told him that "We want you to feel unhampered tactically and strategically to proceed north of the parallel." This was followed by another directive from the Joint Chiefs on October 9, six days before Wake Island, which read:

> In light of the possible intervention of Chinese Communist

forces in North Korea the following . . . is forwarded for your guidance.

Hereafter in the event of the open or covert employment anywhere in Korea of major Communist Chinese units, without prior announcement, you should continue the action as long as, in your judgment, action by forces under your control offers a reasonable chance of success. In any case you will obtain authorization from Washington prior to taking any military action against objectives in Chinese territory.

But as President Truman concluded his optimistic speech at the San Francisco Opera House, none of the many agencies making up the United States intelligence community had discovered any evidence of the open or secret employment of Communist Chinese units. The President returned to Washington thinking that the campaign in Korea was making "excellent progress," and with no solid reason to believe otherwise. He wrote a letter in longhand to MacArthur that read:

"The meeting at Wake Island was a most satisfying one to me. I was pleased with the chance to meet and talk to you about Japan, Korea, and other Far Eastern countries. I was happy to have your views on all the Asiatic situations with which we are faced.

"Our meeting has had a splendid reaction here in the United States, and I think it was well worthwhile if for no other reason than that we became personally acquainted."

Upon his own return from Wake Island to his headquarters on the sixth floor of the *Dai Ichi* ("Number One" or "First") Building in Tokyo, General MacArthur reflected upon the conference. Unlike the President, he had not found it satisfying and felt that its purpose was difficult to diagnose. It made him think that "a curious, and sinister, change was taking place in Washington," and that Truman was weakening in his original courageous decision to defeat communism in Asia.

MacArthur believed in conducting warfare as it had been conducted throughout the ages—"to win"—and he chafed under the restrictions placed upon him by the Administration, even though they allowed the General to exercise a great deal of personal judgment. In fact, the last directive to him of October 9 not only displayed a lack of any serious appreciation of Chinese motives but represented a potentially dangerous derogation of presidential authority to a vigorous theater commander.

Nevertheless, the immediate campaign to destroy the remnants of the fleeing North Korean Army continued to progress well, even though it was unfolding in a state of ambiguity regarding the Chinese and Russians. On October 19, four days after the Wake Island conference, ground troops of the United States 8th Army fought their way into Pyongyang, the North Korean capital. The Americans could see no sign of any Communist Chinese influence whatever in the first Communist capital to be liberated by the United Nations. North Korea was obviously a Soviet satellite and had been since the Russians took over its capital from the Japanese in 1945.

Pictures of Lenin and Stalin could be seen hanging in every house, shop, and office. The Taedong River was now the Lenin River. There was a Soviet commissary on the main thoroughfare, called Stalin Street, and the commissary was stocked with such items as vodka and caviar. The Soviet Embassy was surrounded by two full blocks of houses that had been occupied by Russians, and the capital's largest hotel was referred to simply as the "Russian Hotel." Both the houses and the embassy were abandoned.

On the morning of October 20, General MacArthur was flown the seven hundred miles from Tokyo to a point over Pyongyang where his *SCAP* was joined by an armada of 120 American planes carrying an airborne regiment. As MacArthur watched in his circling plane, 4,100 paratroopers swung down in their multicolored parachutes twenty-five miles north of Pyongyang and sealed off the fleeing North Koreans' escape route.

"It looked perfect to me," the General remarked to a correspondent from *Time* magazine. "It looks like it closed the trap." MacArthur was reminded of a similar maneuver during the Second World War when paratroopers under his command "closed the gap" on the Japanese at Nadzab in New Guinea.

MacArthur was in a jubilant mood as he was flown into the airfield at Pyongyang, where he was greeted by the commander of the 8th Army, Lieutenant General Walton Walker. "Have you got any celebrities here to greet me?" he asked Walker. "What about Kim Buck Too?" Walker had to admit that Kim Il Sung, the Premier of North Korea, had eluded capture.

Before flying back to Tokyo on the afternoon of October 20, MacArthur ordered Walker to send the South Korean forces under his command on an all-out drive toward the Yalu River border between North Korea and Chinese Manchuria. The South Koreans were to be followed by American troops, but the latter were to be held back from coming close to the border so as not to provoke the Chinese or Russians.

With this restriction, in which MacArthur was complying with the Joint Chiefs' directive to him of September 27, the drive north was resumed on October 21. On that day, MacArthur told a press conference in Tokyo: "The war is very definitely coming to an end shortly." *The New York Times* summed up the general feeling that all was going well by informing its readers on October 22: "Four months ago this Wednesday the tank-led columns of the North Korean army moved across the Thirty-Eighth Parallel. Today that army is destroyed and victory for UN forces is at hand in Korea."

In light of the expected victory, the already awesome reputation of General MacArthur shone brighter than ever. His brilliant, and sometimes controversial, military career had had its origins in an age when the United States Cavalry was still fighting Indians. MacArthur, now seventy years old, regarded Korea as "Mars' last gift to an old warrior" and this gift could serve as a fitting capstone to that career.

CHAPTER THREE

The General

Douglas MacArthur was born at the Arsenal Barracks of Little Rock, Arkansas, on January 26, 1880. His father, Captain Arthur MacArthur, was on duty at the Arsenal Barracks at the time. Douglas's mother, Mary Pinkney Hardy, whose own father was a wealthy cotton merchant, came from a Virginia family dating back to the days of the Jamestown colony.

Arthur MacArthur was born at Springfield, Massachusetts, in 1845. Four years later he was taken to Wisconsin, where his father, who practiced law there, was elected Lieutenant Governor of the state. Later he was to become an Associate Justice of the Supreme Court of the District of Columbia. After the Civil War broke out, Arthur MacArthur enlisted in the 24th Wisconsin Volunteer Infantry Regiment in August 1862 at the age of seventeen. Three years later he became a colonel commanding this regiment, the youngest man to hold the rank of colonel in the Union Army.

At the battle of Missionary Ridge, the "Boy Colonel" as he was known to the popular press, led a reckless charge against the Confederate rifle pits at the foot of the ridge, crying to his men, "On Wisconsin!" He was severely wounded in this action, for which he was awarded the Congressional Medal of Honor. After the Civil War, with the reduced rank of captain, Arthur MacArthur served with numerous army commands in the Southwest. His son's first memories were of a march in 1884 from Fort Wingate in New Mexico to Fort Selden in New Mexico, sixty miles above El Paso, Texas. MacArthur's father had been ordered to Fort Selden to guard the fords of the Rio Grande River against Geronimo's attacks and brought his family along on the three-hundred-mile march.

Arthur MacArthur later fought in the Spanish-American War in the Philippines and became the American Military Governor of the islands in 1900. In this command, he had some heated differences over policy with the civilian High Commissioner, William Howard Taft, who was backed by President Theodore Roosevelt. MacArthur was brought home, later passed over for appointment as Army Chief of Staff, and retired in 1909 as a lieutenant general, the senior officer in rank of the army at that time. He died of an apoplectic attack on September 5, 1912, while on the platform addressing a reunion of the 24th Wisconsin veterans in Milwaukee.

While his father was serving at Fort Sam Houston in San Antonio in 1893, Douglas MacArthur entered West Texas Military Academy. His goal was always West Point, which he entered in 1899 after passing a competitive examination. At the academy, he played left field on the baseball team, managed the football team, became First Captain of the Corps, and recorded a four-year scholastic average of 98.14 percent. This remains as one of the highest scholastic averages of any cadet to attend the military academy before or since. His mother, with whom he maintained a close relationship throughout her life, lived near West Point in a hotel during the four years he spent there and encouraged him to believe that he had a destiny to fulfill.

In the opinion of one classmate, Hugh Johnson, later a prominent New Deal official, Cadet MacArthur was the best-looking man he had ever seen. And despite his achievements, MacArthur found time to engage in a few escapades. He was caught publicly kissing a girl on Flirtation Walk, and once slipped out of the horse show in New York City with two other cadets to swagger into Rector's on Broadway, where they ordered three martinis apiece and shook hands with "Diamond Jim" Brady. At his graduation in 1903 as a second lieutenant of engineers, MacArthur was first in his class and the man voted most likely to succeed.

Douglas MacArthur's long involvement in Asian affairs began after his graduation with a short assignment to engineering duties in the Philippines. Then, in October 1904, he joined his father in Japan, where the elder MacArthur had been sent as an American observer in the Russo-Japanese War.

First Lieutenant MacArthur met the important Japanese military leaders and was impressed by the efficiency of their army. On April 30, 1904, the Yalu River—which United Nations troops under MacArthur would approach forty-six years later—was the scene of a minor battle in which the Japanese defeated the Russians. This was the first defeat in modern times of a European army by an Asiatic force.

After observing the Russo-Japanese War, MacArthur, as aide-de-camp to his father, traveled for nine months through India, Java, Siam, Indo-China, and China. This trip deeply impressed him with the coming importance of Asia in world affairs.

In the fall of 1906, Douglas MacArthur returned to Washington and was assigned as aide-de-camp to President Theodore Roosevelt. Other assignments followed, but because of the small size of the military establishment he was still only a captain in April 1914. He then took part in the successful expedition to the Mexican port of Vera Cruz against General Victoriano Huerta. The General had strong-armed his way to power and was causing problems for American interests in Mexico, as Pancho Villa did two years later.

It took United States entry into the war against Germany in April 1917 for MacArthur, now a thirty-seven-year-old major and a member of the general staff, to find a broad stage worthy of his training and talents. He proposed the creation of a "Rainbow" Division, to be made up of National Guard units from twenty-six different states. All of his fellow officers on the general staff opposed the idea, taking the position that only Regular Army units should be sent into action overseas. But MacArthur successfully argued his case over their heads to Secretary of War Newton Baker and President Wilson. In October 1917, he arrived in France as a colonel and Chief of Staff of the Rainbow Division.

MacArthur did not believe in being a desk officer. In one typical engagement at Château-Thierry, he crawled forward with his men in twos and threes through a dark, drizzling night against a nest of German machine guns. These tactics reminded MacArthur of those he had seen used in Indian wars on the frontier. Colonel MacArthur and his men then charged the machine-gun nests with hand grenades and bayonets and cleared them out in hand-to-hand fighting.

Newspaper correspondents took to writing of the dashing MacArthur as the "D'Artagnan of the A.E.F." He was wounded in action, gassed, and among other decorations won two Distinguished Service Crosses, six Silver Stars, and the French Legion of Honor. However, his gallantry had a reckless and melodramatic touch to it that irritated some of his fellow officers.

Reports reached general headquarters that MacArthur, contrary to regulations, wore no iron helmet or gas mask. Further, he carried no arms except a riding crop and refused to command his troops from the rear. These reports were referred to the commander of the American Expeditionary Force, General John J. Pershing, who dismissed them with the remark: "Stop all this nonsense. MacArthur is the greatest leader of troops we have, and I intend to make him a division commander."

Pershing did, and MacArthur ended the war as a brigadier general in command of the Rainbow Division. One of the officers in the division was Captain Harry S. Truman, commander of Battery D, 129th Field Artillery Regiment, Mis-

souri National Guard. While attending Independence High
School, Truman had thought of competing for an appointment
to West Point. However, he was obliged to abandon the idea
when he discovered that his eyesight did not meet the academy's entrance requirements. Truman had worn eyeglasses
since the age of nine to correct poor vision that was worse
than ordinary nearsightedness.

After graduating from high school in 1901 as an average
student, Truman did not go on to college but instead went
to work immediately. His first important job was as a time-
keeper for the L. J. Smith Construction Company in the
summer of 1902. Later, he tried farming, zinc mining, and
oil speculation with indifferent success. But he retained his
interest in military life and became a charter member of the
Missouri National Guard in 1905, when he was twenty-five.
In France, Captain Truman commanded his artillery battery
in various sectors of the front from August 20, 1918, to the
Armistice of November 11 of that year. During his service
with the Rainbow Division, Captain Truman had no occasion to meet its commanding general, Douglas MacArthur.

Upon his return to civilian life, the thirty-five-year-old
captain retained his commission in the Missouri National
Guard and opened a haberdashery store in the fall of 1919
near the corner of Twelfth and Baltimore streets in Kansas
City. His partner was former sergeant Eddie Jacobson, with
whom Truman had operated a financially successful military
canteen for the National Guard.

When MacArthur returned to a peacetime United States
in April 1919, he found the experience somewhat anti-
climactic. Arriving in New York City on the liner *Leviathan,*
he was distressed to see no welcoming crowds waiting at the
dock to cheer his men. He watched them march off in silence
and thought that this was "a sad, gloomy end of the Rainbow."

MacArthur's next major assignment was to West Point.
At thirty-eight, he was the youngest American division commander in Europe. In June 1919, at the age of thirty-nine,
he became the youngest superintendent the military academy

had ever had. But his attempts to modernize West Point and to prepare its cadets for another major war that few thought would ever come were marked by a series of frustrating wrangles with Congress over money.

The jazz age of the roaring twenties was not a time when soldiers cast in the heroic mold were appreciated or needed in America. By January 1920, the army was down to a peacetime low of 130,000 men, ranking seventeenth in terms of numbers in the world's armies. In 1922, at the age of forty-two, MacArthur married for the first time. Until now, he had relied for feminine companionship largely on his mother, who lived with him most of the time and who, during World War I, had written letters urging his advancement to her friend, General Pershing.

The new Mrs. MacArthur was the former Louise Cromwell Brooks. She was the stepdaughter of Edward T. Stotesbury, a financier with a reported personal fortune of more than 100 million dollars and a partner in J. P. Morgan and Company. Louise had been divorced in 1919 from Walter Brooks, a wealthy Baltimore contractor and socialite, by whom she had had two children. Although she considered her husband "the handsomest man I had ever seen," Louise's interests in high society in Baltimore and New York did not make her an ideal army wife. She and MacArthur had no children and were divorced on June 18, 1929, in Reno, while he was stationed in Manila. The General ascribed the divorce to "mutual incompatibility." Louise declared that they were "wholly incompatible to each other," later adding that it was "an interfering mother-in-law who eventually succeeded in disrupting our married life."

After concluding his assignment at West Point in 1922, MacArthur was assigned to the Philippines to command the Military District of Manila. He returned to the United States in 1925 and for the next three years successively commanded the IV Corps Area with headquarters in Atlanta and the III Corps Area with headquarters in Baltimore. He went back to Manila in 1928 and commanded the Philippine Department until 1930 when he was appointed Army Chief of Staff by President Herbert Hoover. At fifty, MacArthur was the youngest man ever to occupy that post.

But the gray Depression era with its 10 million unemployed had now replaced the frivolous jazz age. This was also an inauspicious time for a soldier capable of great things. MacArthur gave speeches designed to combat pacificism and the "Red Menace," but the United States Army was called upon to fight only one engagement while he was Chief of Staff. On July 28, 1932, at the request of President Hoover, and with the assistance of two majors, George Patton and Dwight Eisenhower, General MacArthur directed the Regular Army's rout of the Bonus Marchers. This disgruntled band of some twenty-five thousand unemployed and unarmed American veterans had been encamped in and around Washington for two months. They demanded the immediate payment by the Federal Government of a cash bonus for their services in World War I.

During the afternoon of July 28, MacArthur had the veterans ousted from downtown Washington. When the Bonus Marchers fled over the Eleventh Street Bridge to their shabby camp in the Anacostia Flats, President Hoover sent word to MacArthur through Secretary of War Patrick Hurley that he did not want the army to cross the bridge in pursuit of the veterans.

The Chief of Staff ignored the presidential order, remarking to his special aide, Major Eisenhower, that he was "too busy and did not want either himself or his staff bothered by people coming down [to the bridge] and pretending to bring orders." That night, the regular troops charged across the bridge and sent the disorganized Bonus Marchers fleeing into Maryland.

President Hoover did not reprimand his Chief of Staff for what amounted to insubordination. Shortly after the event, MacArthur told the press: "It is my opinion that had the President not acted today, had he permitted the thing to go on for twenty-four hours more, he would have been faced with a grave situation which would have caused a real battle. Had he let it go on another week I believe that the institutions of our government would have been severely threatened."

For his successful if somewhat brutal action against what he described as an "army of disillusioned and lost men" whom he considered misguided and mainly led by Communists, MacArthur received some praise. "He is the man of the hour," declared Secretary of War Hurley. The General was also criticized by many liberals. It was said that he had used more force than the situation had called for and that there was no need for a Chief of Staff to personally direct a local riot-control operation in full uniform. Major Eisenhower had advised him that it would be "highly inappropriate" for the head of the army to accompany the evicting force. Eisenhower also suggested that it "would be the better part of wisdom, if not of valor, to avoid meeting" newspaper correspondents after the operation was completed.

MacArthur declined both suggestions and in speaking to the correspondents about "a bad-looking mob . . . animated by the essence of revolution" he laid himself open to justified charges of miscalculation and impulsiveness. For a later investigation by the Veterans Bureau indicated that 94 percent of the Bonus Marchers were genuine veterans motivated by the hard times that had befallen them. A Red conspiracy was a product of MacArthur's imagination.

He was always extremely touchy about any kind of criticism, and he reacted to the Bonus Army episode by writing: "The most extravagant distortions of what had occurred were widely circulated. I was violently attacked, and even blatantly misrepresented before Congress. Speeches pictured me in full dress uniform astride a fiery white charger, bedecked with medals, waving a bloody saber, and leading a mad cavalry charge against unarmed and innocent citizens. Of course there was absolutely no foundation for such statements."

Nevertheless, tanks and gas bombs, as well as cavalrymen wielding sabers under the command of Major Patton had been employed against a civilian mob, and MacArthur had directed a street battle dressed in burnished boots with spurs, pink breeches, and a field tunic whose left breast was covered with rows of ribbons. The Chief of Staff had asked his intelligence to furnish proof that the Bonus Marchers or at least their leaders were Communists. When this was not forthcoming, he was able to convince himself that many of the marchers were not even veterans. The affair was a long way from the battlefields of France, which had provided a more fitting stage for the "D'Artagnan of the A.E.F."

Upon succeeding Herbert Hoover in 1933, Franklin Roosevelt nevertheless thought highly enough of MacArthur to reappoint him Chief of Staff. The General did not hesitate to argue with the new President about reductions in military appropriations. During one such exchange in 1934, Roosevelt, according to MacArthur, "turned the full vials of his sarcasm upon me. He was a scorcher when aroused."

Tension began to boil over within the General. A paralyzing nausea crept over him. But he stood his ground and offered his resignation. It was not accepted by the President. Conciliatory words were spoken. But after leaving the White House, MacArthur vomited on its steps.

The President once told MacArthur: "Douglas, I think you are our best general, but I believe you would be our worst politician." To one of his chief aides, Rexford Tugwell, Roosevelt had said in 1932 that Senator Huey Long of Louisiana and General MacArthur were the two most dangerous men in the United States. What Roosevelt feared was the possibility of the people losing faith in the democratic process if the severe problems of the Depression were not solved. They might then turn to a strong man to save them—to a movement led from the left by the Louisiana Kingfish with his radical "share-the-wealth" program or to a movement led from the conservative right by General MacArthur.

Upon completing his tour of duty as Chief of Staff in 1935, MacArthur left the United States and returned to the Philippines at the request of its President, Manuel Quezon, to organize an effective defense for the islands against possible

Japanese invasion. Except for a brief trip in 1937, he would not return to America for the next fourteen years.

The General was only fifty-five when he left Washington. After his meteoric rise to Chief of Staff, there was really no suitable command for him within the continental United States. He did not want to retire, for a business career did not interest him and, since he was a Republican, a political career offered little promise in an era dominated by Franklin Roosevelt and the New Deal.

So, as Military Adviser to the Philippine Government, Mac-Arthur became an expatriate living in an air-conditioned penthouse atop the Manila Hotel. In August 1936, Quezon made him Field Marshal of the Philippine Army. In filling this role, MacArthur had designed a sharkskin uniform with black trousers and a white coat resplendent with stars, braid, and unique lapel ornamentations. Major Eisenhower, although he preferred a troop command, came to the Philippines in 1935 at MacArthur's insistence to serve for four years as his chief of staff. The unpretentious Eisenhower tried to dissuade his chief from accepting the title of field marshal on the grounds that it was "pompous and rather ridiculous to be the field marshal of a virtually nonexisting army." Eisenhower's suggestion was not accepted. On December 31, 1937, MacArthur officially retired from the United States Army and continued as military adviser to the Philippine Government in a private status.

MacArthur was constantly irked by the fact that the Roosevelt Administration, beset with the problems of solving the Depression, could not supply the men and matériel that the General believed were required by the Philippine Army and the small U.S. Army garrison in the islands. Nevertheless, MacArthur displayed unwarranted confidence in his ability to defend the Philippines against Japanese invasion. In mid-May 1941, he told the writer John Hersey that "if Japan entered the war, the Americans, the British and the Dutch could handle her with about half the forces they now have deployed in the Far East." The field marshal did not believe that the Japanese would attack before the spring of 1942 in any case. On November 28, 1941, George C. Marshall, Army Chief of Staff, replied to an optimistic message from MacArthur: "The Secretary of War and I were highly pleased to receive your report that your command is ready for any eventuality."

This report did not turn out to be correct. Ten hours after attacking Pearl Harbor, the Japanese sent bombers flying over Clark Field, fifty miles northeast of Manila. The Japanese caught seventeen B-17 bombers, almost half of MacArthur's heavy air force, on the ground and destroyed them. The surprise attack also destroyed any chance of preventing the Japanese ground invasion of the Philippines.

When it became apparent that the Bataan Peninsula could not be defended by his outnumbered forces, MacArthur was ordered to Australia by President Roosevelt. Now recalled to active duty as Commanding General, U.S. Army, Far East, MacArthur left the island fortress of Corregidor at the entrance to Manila Bay on March 11, 1942. After a hazardous journey in a PT boat to the island of Mindanao in the southern Philippines, he was flown from there to Australia to take command of Allied forces for the counteroffensive against Japan. One of his primary purposes, he announced to the press, was the relief of the Philippines. "I came through," MacArthur said, "and I shall return."

For his stand in the Philippines and escape from the islands, MacArthur was awarded the decoration that had thus far eluded him and which his father had won in the Civil War— the Congressional Medal of Honor. Another military figure might have fallen into obscurity after the disaster in the Philippines, but MacArthur's heroic pose in the midst of defeat and his confident speeches about eventual victory struck a responsive chord with the American people that was recognized by President Roosevelt. But Roosevelt gave MacArthur's theater second place to the requirements of the European theater as the General launched his counteroffensive against Japan in New Guinea in the fall of 1942.

MacArthur never admitted the logic behind this Europe-first strategy. But after the long years of the jazz age, the Depression, and expatriation in the Philippines, he came into his own in the Southwest Pacific. By the fall of 1944, troops under his command, working with the Navy in a series of skillful island-hopping maneuvers, had advanced 1500 miles from the jungles of New Guinea back to the Philippines. On October 20, MacArthur waded ashore to the beachhead at Leyte, took a microphone in hand, and announced as the rains came down and Japanese soldiers still moved through bushes a few hundred yards away: "People of the Philippines: I have returned. . . . Rally to me. . . ." Then, on September 2, 1945, he strode onto the quarterdeck of the battleship *Missouri* in Tokyo Bay, sat down at a plain table covered with documents, and accepted the surrender of the Japanese Imperial Forces as Supreme Commander for Allied Powers—the United States, China, United Kingdom, Soviet Union, Australia, Canada, France, the Netherlands, and New Zealand.

Instead of returning to the United States and a hero's welcome, MacArthur chose to remain in Japan to direct that country's occupation and postwar rehabilitation as what amounted to the American proconsul in the Pacific. He established his headquarters in the Dai Ichi Building in Tokyo across from the moat surrounding the Emperor's Palace and took up permanent residence in the American Embassy a mile and a quarter away.

MacArthur lived in the embassy with his second wife, the former Jean Marie Faircloth, a wealthy native of Murfrees-boro, Tennessee, whom he had married in 1937, and their son, Arthur, who was born in Manila in 1938. Mrs. Mac-Arthur, who was nineteen years younger than her husband, always addressed him as "General"; the marriage appeared to be a very happy one.

In Tokyo, the General rarely varied from a fixed routine. He rose late, was driven to the Dai Ichi Building around 11 A.M., worked until around 2 P.M., then was driven back to the embassy for lunch and a nap. He then returned to the

Dai Ichi Building around 5 or 5:30 P.M. and worked until
9 P.M.—sometimes later. He worked seven days a week, including Christmas Day and all other holidays, and did not
miss a day because of illness. Between September 1945 and
the outbreak of the Korean War in June 1950, he had left
Tokyo or its environs only twice. Although retaining firm
control of the occupation, MacArthur kept himself personally
aloof; since assuming the role of Supreme Commander for
Allied Powers, he had spoken with only sixteen Japanese
more than twice, and these were all major figures such as the
Emperor or Premier or Chief Justice.

To MacArthur, the occupation of Japan and America's
role in Asia were of vital importance. Asia was where about
60 percent of humanity now lived. By the year 2000, Asia's
population would be more than ten times that of the United
States. America would face across the Pacific almost 4 billion
people, who would have mastered most of the then existing
technology.

MacArthur felt that it was in Asia where the "history of
the next 10,000 years would be written." He considered
Europe to be "a dying system," although Europe still occupied most of the attention of the United States Government
in the years following World War II.

The occupation of Japan was, in the opinion of most observers, another MacArthur success. During a visit to Tokyo,
former President Herbert Hoover referred to his onetime
Army Chief of Staff as "the reincarnation of Saint Paul." *The
New York Times* commented: "General MacArthur's administration is a model of government and a boon to peace in
the Far East. He has swept away an autocratic regime by a
warrior god and installed in its place a democratic government presided over by a very human emperor and based on
the will of the people as expressed in free elections."

Other Western nations encountered severe difficulties in
postwar Asia: the French in Indochina, the Dutch in Indo-
nesia, the British in Hong Kong, Burma, Singapore, and
Ceylon. But as almost nowhere else in Asia, things went

smoothly in Japan. Korea was not part of MacArthur's command. In 1945, the occupying Japanese surrendered the industrial north of that country to Soviet forces and the agricultural south to the United States. In 1948, Russian and American forces withdrew and separate sovereign republics were established in the north and south.

In the early morning hours of June 25, 1950, MacArthur was sleeping when the telephone rang in his darkened bedroom in the American Embassy. He answered its urgent ringing, and the headquarters duty officer told him that at four o'clock that morning the Communist North Koreans had attacked in great strength south across the 38th Parallel.

MacArthur experienced an uncanny nightmare feeling. The same thing had happened to him on a Sunday morning nine years before, at the same hour. Then, he had been awakened by a telephone call in his Manila penthouse telling him that Japanese bombers were attacking Clark Field. Then, as now, he had not proven to be a better forecaster than anyone else. Both attacks took him by surprise.

But the General went into action with characteristic vigor. He was authorized by Washington to use the U.S. Air Force and Navy to assist the South Korea defense. However, after a flying visit in hazardous weather from Tokyo to South Korea on June 29, he saw that the situation bordered on disaster. The next day he reported to Washington that the only hope of saving the Republic of Korea from Communist aggression was the immediate use of American ground troops. Once having been told of MacArthur's opinion, President Truman instructed Secretary of the Army Frank Pace to send in the ground troops.

MacArthur used them skillfully, committing them piecemeal into the battle. He planned an unorthodox delaying retreat to a beachhead at Pusan in the southeast corner of the Korean Peninsula and built up the strength of his forces behind the one-hundred-by-five-hundred-mile rectangle of the Pusan perimeter.

Then, in a masterstroke, MacArthur sent the U.S. First

Marine Division storming ashore on September 15 at Inchon, a port on Korea's west coast 150 miles in the enemy's rear. The next day, United Nations infantry broke out of the Pusan perimeter and shortly linked up with the Marines at Inchon, cutting the enemy's lines in two and almost destroying him between two jaws of a massive pincers.

As a result, by the time the Wake Island Conference took place on October 15, United Nations forces controlled the entire Korean Peninsula south of the 38th Parallel. Inchon was reminiscent of the enveloping amphibious landings that MacArthur had employed to defeat Japan. But it was more than a daring military success. It also added further to the legend of MacArthur's infallibility.

For the plain fact was that while the United States Navy and Marine Corps had executed the Inchon operation, MacArthur had conceived and pushed it through against the opposition of his own headquarters staff in Tokyo and the Joint Chiefs of Staff in Washington. This opposition was summed up by the Chief of Naval Operations, Admiral Forrest Sherman, with the observation: "If every possible geographic and naval handicap were listed—Inchon has 'em all."

MacArthur had not been unused to arguing with the Navy about strategy in World War II. Admiral Sherman went to Tokyo, along with the Army Chief of Staff, J. Lawton Collins, in an attempt to talk MacArthur out of Inchon. They were not successful. At a final preinvasion meeting in Tokyo with a group of still dubious admirals and generals, the Supreme Commander told them: "I realize that Inchon is a 5000-to-1 gamble, but I am used to taking such odds." His voice dropped so that his audience had to strain to hear him. "We shall land at Inchon and I shall crush them."

That is what happened, and it was not difficult to understand why such strokes caused MacArthur to be held in high regard by his subordinates. To Lieutenant General George Stratemeyer, Commanding General, Far East Air Force, he was "the greatest man alive." To MacArthur's chief of staff,

Major General Edward Almond, he was "the greatest man in history." Major General Courtney Whitney thought that he was a "brilliant" man of "titanic influence."

Whitney, fifty-three years old, was a native of Takoma Park, Maryland, and a 1923 graduate of the Law School of National University. From 1927 to 1940 he practiced law successfully in Manila. In May 1943, he joined MacArthur in Brisbane, Australia, and stayed at his side through the occupation of Japan, where he served as chief deputy in charge of the government section of the Supreme Command for Allied Powers. Whitney was probably MacArthur's closest personal friend. However, not everyone admired Major General Whitney, who had been promoted one grade after the Wake Island meeting by President Truman to please MacArthur. Major Faubion Bowers, another MacArthur aide who was fluent in Japanese, considered Whitney a "fat, puffy" man who was "one of the most cordially detested officials of the occupation."

When the United Nations forces moved north across the 38th Parallel and captured the North Korean capital of Pyongyang on October 19, the only realistic obstacle to the complete occupation of Korea lay in the Chinese Communist threats to intervene in the limited war. General Whitney never denied that his chief had told President Truman at Wake Island that there was very little likelihood of Chinese intervention. But Whitney thought that MacArthur had given this estimate on the assumption that he would be allowed to retaliate against the Chinese with full force if they did act.

MacArthur had followed the Chinese Communist problem closely since the original North Korean attack in June. His information about the Chinese came primarily from the military intelligence section, G-2, of his own staff. He had the greatest confidence in its chief, Major General Charles Willoughby. While not actively excluding other intelligence agencies from the Far East, such as the Central Intelligence Agency, MacArthur preferred to rely on his own men. This had served him well in the past.

Willoughby, sixty-eight years old, tall, and barrel-chested, spoke English with a marked Central European accent. He had been born in Heidelberg, the son of an American mother and a German aristocrat named Tscheppe-Weidenbach. Willoughby assumed his mother's maiden name upon becoming a naturalized American citizen in 1910. He entered the Army as a private and was a captain teaching military history at Fort Leavenworth in the mid-1930's when he first met MacArthur. The General summoned him to the Philippines before the Japanese invasion, and Willoughby, who also spoke Spanish and Japanese with a Teutonic accent, had served him as G-2 ever since.

To MacArthur, "no commander was ever better served" than by such staff members as Willoughby. The G-2 was a member of the so-called "Bataan Gang," which had formed a loyal inner circle of admirers around the General since the early Philippine days and whose unquestioning adulation might serve to shield him from unpleasant realities. John Gunther once asked Willoughby what had chiefly impressed him about MacArthur at their first meeting and was told: "Not just his shiny boots."

General Willoughby labored under difficulties in trying to discover what was really going on in the far north of Korea. After the American occupation of South Korea ended in 1948, native spy networks disintegrated. Attempts to replace them were made impossible by the North Korean invasion. American aerial reconnaissance capabilities were weakened by the drastic reduction in these services that followed World War II. In any case, there were few accurate maps of North Korea with which aerial photographs could be compared.

General Willoughby's principal source of information concerning Chinese Communist military activity on the Manchurian side of the Yalu River border came from the Nationalist Chinese on Formosa who maintained contacts with the mainland. This information was reasonably accurate. Since June, Willoughby had compiled a succession of comments and reports on the gradual buildup of Chinese Communist troops in Manchuria. His "Daily Intelligence Summaries" were made available to the Pentagon, Allied liaison officers in Tokyo, and the United Nations General Assembly. These intelligence summaries, of course, described what the Chinese Communists could do, not what they would do.

As early as August 31, two months after the war began, the Daily Intelligence Summary of the Far East Command reported:

> Troop movements from Central China to Manchuria over a considerable period suggest preliminary to entering the Korean theater. Total Chinese strength in Manchuria estimated to be 246,000 Regular and 374,000 Militia security forces.

In early October, General Willoughby estimated that thirty-eight regular Chinese Communist divisions were stationed in Manchuria. These numbered about a third of a million men. The day before the Wake Island Conference, he noted that twenty-four of these divisions were massed at crossing points along the Yalu River. Concerning the Chinese leaders' threats to send those troops across the Yalu into North Korea, Willoughby admitted that this was "beyond the purview of combat intelligence." However, MacArthur's G-2 did go on record as estimating that the threats were "probably in the category of diplomatic blackmail."

General MacArthur was operating as though he fully agreed with this estimate. On October 19, four days after Wake Island, Operation Plan 202 was issued by Far East Command Headquarters. It provided for the removal of United Nations forces from Korea upon the successful conclusion of hostilities. Plan 202 was based on the assumption that "there would be no intervention either by Chinese or Soviet forces."

Such thinking was shared by the State Department, which came to the conclusion on the same day that Plan 202 was issued that Chinese intervention was "unlikely." This was a repetition of the estimate that Secretary of State Dean Acheson had given to the United Nations General Assembly on October 4.

This guesswork ignored the significance of a curious incident that had taken place on October 12. That day, nine Chinese soldiers were captured by the South Koreans, although not in battle. Some of the Chinese had simply walked into the South Korean lines. Others had been discovered in hiding places that were not well concealed. The Chinese wore uniforms resembling those of the North Koreans, but without insignia of rank or unit. The Chinese talked freely, explaining to intelligence officers that they were volunteers and that only nine thousand of them were fighting with the North Korean People's Army.

However, by October 24 there was still no evidence of large-scale Chinese intervention. On that date, MacArthur's forces were about seventy-five miles away from the Manchurian border. So he ordered his commanders to "drive forward with all speed and full utilization of their forces."

The Pentagon was "stunned" by the order, according to Dean Acheson. For it violated the September 27 directive of the Joint Chiefs of Staff to MacArthur that "No non-Korean ground forces will be used in the area along the Manchurian border." Moreover, the General issued his new order without prior notification to Washington.

However, instead of issuing a definite order restraining MacArthur, the Joint Chiefs cabled him asking for a report on his reasoning "since the action contemplated was a matter of concern to them." The United Nations Commander cabled back that he intended to send American troops into areas bordering on China "as a matter of military necessity." He felt that the South Koreans lacked the strength and leadership necessary to handle the situation. Furthermore, he could see no conflict between his order and previous directives from Washington.

The Joint Chiefs accepted this explanation. Why they did so can perhaps be explained by MacArthur's advantage over them in age, accomplishment, experience, and apparent military wisdom. General Bradley, Chairman of the Joint Chiefs, later admitted that they felt literally incapacitated to deal with MacArthur because his stature was so great. A less kind interpretation would be that the Joint Chiefs were playing the old army game of not bucking the system and following the leader.

The fact was that Bradley's battle experience was all in the European theater during World War II, and he was thirteen years junior to MacArthur. Before he became Army Chief of Staff, J. Lawton Collins, known as "Lightning Joe," had been commander of the 25th ("Tropic Lightning") Division on Guadalcanal and leader of the breakthrough at Saint-Lô after the Normandy Invasion. But Lightning Joe had only been a first lieutenant when MacArthur was Army Chief of Staff in the early 1930's. During that period, Admiral Forrest Sherman, Chief of Naval Operations, had been a junior lieutenant commander. The Air Force Chief of Staff, Hoyt Vandenberg, was a West Point cadet when MacArthur was superintendent of the military academy.

The Joint Chiefs did have a military superior who possessed enough stature and official power to deal firmly with MacArthur. He was George Catlett Marshall, Secretary of Defense, who had been called out of retirement by President Truman in September. After graduating from Virginia Military Institute in 1901, Marshall had served as an army officer in China from 1924 to 1927, was the United States ambassador to that country from November 1945 to January 1947, and Secretary of State from the latter date until 1949, when ill health caused his resignation. Based on this long experience, Marshall might have been expected to have a more serious appreciation of what the Chinese were up to than anyone else.

Like MacArthur, Marshall was a five-star General of the Army, having attained that rank when he served as Army Chief of Staff throughout World War II. However, Marshall

had almost been sidetracked from undertaking his distinguished career in 1933. He had then incurred MacArthur's
displeasure and was virtually exiled by him to Chicago, where
Marshall marked time for three stultifying years as Senior
Instructor of the National Guard until MacArthur finished his
tour as Chief of Staff and went to the Philippines.

As Army Chief of Staff in World War II, Marshall had
to deal with many priorities and demanding command per-
sonalities. He found MacArthur, who felt that the Navy
wanted to assume general command control of all operations
in the Pacific and relegate the Army to a subsidiary role,
"supersensitive about everything" and a man who "thought
everybody had ulterior motives about everything." Marshall
later reminisced, "With Chennault in China and MacArthur
in the Southwest Pacific, I sure had a combination of
temperament."

Now Marshall was supervising MacArthur again, but he,
like the Joint Chiefs, did not advise President Truman to
restrain the recent winner of the 5000-to-1 gamble at Inchon.
And so the United Nations forces continued to advance toward
the Manchurian border through the third week of October,
1950, which fell in the Year of the Tiger on the Chinese
calendar. South Korean officers of the advance spearheads
reported back to 8th Army headquarters: "We will not stop
until we bathe our sabers in the Yalu River."

The Americans who followed the confident South Koreans
were not prepared to fight a rugged, old-fashioned infantry
war. Such wars were believed to have ended five years before
when the mushroom clouds arose over Hiroshima and Naga-
saki. And so, in a spirit of wishful thinking and blind optimism, the U.N. commanders moved their forces north. The
decision to do so was made in secret debate within the inner
circle of the American Government, and only faint echoes
reached out to the American people, who had the most stake
in the outcome.

There was no great debate in Congress as to the wisdom of

the northward drive. But then there is no reason to believe that such a debate would have produced a greater respect for Chinese capabilities or their indirect warnings. The Chinese were simply not taken seriously, a throwback to the days before the Communist takeover when a sign was posted prominently at the gates to the foreign compound in Shanghai: "No dogs or Chinese."

CHAPTER
FOUR

Lying in Wait

There had been unusual activity along the Yalu River on the night of October 14. But no South Korean soldiers or spies or American agents were there to report on it.

On that night, soldiers began to march in double time across some of the Yalu's twelve international bridges into North Korea from South Manchuria. The soldiers moved silently on the crepe-rubber soles of their canvas shoes. They were not accompanied by tanks or trucks or any other vehicles whose noise might betray their presence.

At daybreak of October 15, as President Truman's plane approached Wake Island, the movement south abruptly stopped. During the daylight hours, as General MacArthur was assuring President Truman that the Korean War would be over by Thanksgiving and that there was "very little" possibility of the Chinese entering it, the bridges remained empty and quiet.

As soon as darkness fell, the marching resumed. The soldiers were not Russian, but Chinese. General Nieh Jung-chen had not been bluffing or attempting diplomatic blackmail when he told Indian Ambassador Panikkar back on September 25 that China would not "sit back with folded hands and let the Americans come to the border." This was a warning that was meant to be taken seriously, as were the subsequent warnings of Chou En-lai.

The Chinese private soldier who marched in darkness into North Korea was not a volunteer but a member of the regular People's Liberation Army. He usually wore a mustard-yellow, heavily quilted cotton uniform. His head and neck were protected by a cotton cap with fur-lined ear flaps. In his small pack was a four-day supply of food, usually consisting of soybeans, rice, or millet. After finishing this meager ration, he was for the most part expected to live off the land.

There was no complaining about forced night marching, for the Chinese was a semiliterate peasant born to hardship. He knew nothing about democracy, for he did not live in a democracy now and had not lived in one under Chiang Kai-shek. Frequently louse-ridden, he was not inoculated against plague and other diseases under any organized medical system. There was no provision for his discharge from the People's Liberation Army. Once recruited, he was expected to remain under arms until killed or rendered physically unfit for service. He carried with him over the Yalu bridges a strange assortment of weapons. Rifles were mostly Japanese, confiscated by the Russians after they occupied Manchuria in 1945 and in turn given to the Chinese Communists.

Other rifles were American, as were most of the carbines, pistols, bazookas, automatic rifles, and heavy and light machine guns. These weapons had been supplied by the United States to the Chinese Nationalists during the Chinese civil war. The Chinese Communists had confiscated them after their victory and Chiang's flight to Formosa (Taiwan) in 1949.

The Chinese infantryman who crossed the Yalu carried with him only a few Soviet-made weapons, such as grenades and submachine guns. Below the battalion level, the Chinese communicated with each other by means of runners, the lighting of colored flares, or the sounding of whistles, horns, or bugles.

The weapons and the communications system of the People's Liberation Army were primitive by Western standards. But they did work. And senior officers were skilled and experienced in defeating forces of superior firepower and technical expertise. In fighting the Japanese and the Chinese Nationalists, they had mastered the tactical doctrines of mobility, ambush, and sudden surprise attack followed by a quick withdrawal, and the use of hostile terrain as an ally. The senior officers had all absorbed Mao Tse-tung's written maxim of 1938: "We have always advocated the policy of luring the enemy to penetrate deep because this is the most effective military policy for a weak army in strategic defense against a strong army."

The Yalu River, which separates China from Korea, rises in the mountains of northeastern Korea. Then the river flows westward for five hundred miles, mostly through a gorgelike channel rimmed by high mountains, before emptying into the Yellow Sea. Electricity generated at many dams and reservoirs on the Yalu and its tributaries provided the basic supply of power for North Korean and Manchurian mining and manufacturing. Manchuria had the richest agricultural resources in China and was that country's most highly developed industrial region, largely as a result of the Japanese occupation from 1931 to 1945. For these practical reasons, Peking might well be concerned about an advance of foreign armies toward the Yalu River.

Twelve international bridges linked Manchuria with North Korea. The Chinese infantryman who crossed these bridges did so only in small, compact units. Once across, the Chinese were met by North Korean Communist guides and could always expect more cooperation from the local populace than any Westerner.

Following their guides, the Chinese saw in North Korea tall mountain ranges capped with thick forests that isolated one part of the countryside from the other. Sheer granite cliffs often dropped off from the mountains. There were no roads along the summit ridges and ravines. Such roads as did exist in the valleys were winding trails so narrow that the Chinese had to walk them in slow single file.

In the valleys, the Chinese were greeted by the characteristic aroma of Korea—the stench of human excrement stored in leaky "honey wagons," barrels, and pails for use as soil fertilizer. This aroma always vanished in late November when snow blanketed the land with ten-foot-high drifts and subzero temperatures froze the Yalu and the land surrounding it to the hardness of rock.

Once in North Korea, the Chinese were led by their guides to assembly areas. Relays of North Korean porters carried on their backs what little heavy equipment the Chinese had brought with them. When day broke, the Chinese stopped marching and hid in forests, caves, tunnels, farmhouses, or whatever other cover was available.

The Chinese did not move from their cover during daylight. They rested and listened to lectures by political officers and to instructions from military officers. But when darkness fell, the Chinese marched off to their next objective. They covered nearly twenty miles in a night's march, which equaled the brutal marching pace of the Roman legions. If they were, infrequently, obliged to march in daylight, the Chinese infantryman obeyed orders to halt and stand motionless if an aircraft appeared overhead. Any man who moved was shot down by an officer.

United States intelligence missed detecting this Chinese movement into North Korea. There were, however, reasons for the failure. The Chinese Nationalists on Formosa who had supplied General Willoughby with information about the troop buildup in Manchuria came up with nothing concrete about the crossing of the Yalu. To report on this development, Willoughby had no network of native agents. Such aerial reconnaissance as could be undertaken revealed nothing. The Chinese hid from aerial cameras during the day and marched at night when the cameras could detect them only if the moon were unnaturally bright.

In any case, the Air Force of 1950 had not one expert qualified in the art of photo interpretation. Some photographs were taken that revealed forest fires in North Korea. Nothing unusual was interpreted from these photographs. The fires had in fact been set by the Chinese to serve as smokescreens for their infrequent daylight movements.

And so the Chinese marched over the Yalu bridges like phantoms in the night and disappeared in the mountains of North Korea. They were all regular soldiers and officers of the twenty-three-year-old People's Liberation Army. Many of them had been working in various parts of China on economic development projects before being deployed to Manchuria and had been put through a two- to three-month period of special combat training and political indoctrination. Except for anti-American propaganda, there was no consistency in the indoctrination. In an effort to maintain secrecy, some of the ordinary soldiers were not told why they were going to Korea until just before they crossed the Yalu. Others were not told until they had crossed the river. All were told that the South Koreans had started the war.

The Chinese units were organized so that they were composed of men from the same villages or regions, because of the variety of dialects and subcultures of China. The average Manchurian could not understand the soldier from Shanghai, the Cantonese the pure Mandarin dialect of North China. Men from Mongolia or Sinkiang knew little Mandarin at all, which was the dialect favored by staff officers.

This varied assortment of men was not motivated to fight by material rewards. The monthly pay of a private was roughly forty-one cents a month and that of a division commander was about one dollar and thirty cents. Neither were the ordinary soldiers motivated by the beatings so common in the old warlord armies. Instead, Communist political officers exhorted the men to fight bravely to defend China from the imperialist aggressor and to win awards and honors for themselves and their families. Precombat meetings usually ended with squad members taking and affixing their thumb prints to oaths like this one:

A SOLEMN PLEDGE TO KILL THE ENEMY

We eight members of the squad hereby solemnly promise to be determined to kill the enemy by helping the leader in this combat and achieve merits to our most glorious honor.

(1) I will fight bravely without being afraid of enemy fire and make our firearms effective to the greatest extent.

(2) I will overcome every difficulty. I will not be afraid of great mountains to cross or of long marches. I will fight bravely as usual even when I have nothing to eat for a full day.

(3) We will be united and help one another, observe one another, so that we may not retreat even a step.

(4) We eight members of our squad without fail will kill and wound more than three enemies for the people of China and Korea and for our leader.

(5) Should we fail to do these, we wish to be punished.

The Chinese soldiers were organized into basic infantry squads that had one noteworthy feature: the "three-by-three" structure. This structure facilitated surveillance and control by the squad leader, normally a Communist Party member, and provided tactical control at the lowest level. General James Van Fleet, after he assumed command of the 8th Army in April 1951, would have reason to write of the effectiveness of the "three-by-three" device:

The Red Chinese Army is divided at the very bottom into units of three men, with each assigned to watch the others and aware that they in turn are watching him. Even when one of them goes to the latrine, the other two follow. No soldier dares fail to obey orders or even complain. . . . The little teams of three, each man warily watching the others, begin the advance. . . . Yet—although terribly alone in the fight despite the two men at his side, made even more lonely by the doubt whether the two are there to help him or to spy on him—the Red soldier moves ever forward. . . ."

These soldiers of the People's Liberation Army [PLA] formed a semiguerrilla infantry force that would have been slaughtered on the conventional open battlefields of Europe. For the PLA had few tanks and no heavy artillery, air force, atom bomb, or capability to mount operations combining land, sea, and air arms. These obvious weaknesses were not conducive to leading General MacArthur, the Pentagon, or the State Department to take seriously the danger signals of the Chinese Communist threats to intervene in Korea.

Moreover, Western observers who had studied Chinese history of the past century had no reason to be impressed by Chinese military ability. Ever since Great Britain had easily won the Opium War of 1839–1842, exposing China's military impotence and ending her long isolation, the rulers of what had been "The Middle Kingdom," the center of the world, had been repeatedly defeated and humiliated whenever engaged in conventional battle by the Western "barbarians" and the Japanese "dwarfs" as well.

In the traditional Chinese system of values, the professional soldier was not highly esteemed. He ranked below the scholar, farmer, artisan, and merchant in the social hierarchy. "Good iron is not used to make a nail nor a good man to make a soldier" was the dogma perpetuated by Chinese scholars and civilian chroniclers.

Western observers had long tended to place a low assessment on the Chinese as a fighting man. Typical was an analysis by Colonel John Magruder, U.S. Army military attaché in Peiping. In 1931, Colonel Magruder wrote: "A glance at Chinese history is proof of the characteristic flavor of Chinese pacifism. . . . The Chinese have no military history worthy of scientific study." And indeed this history did conjure up images of plundering bandit hordes, venal warlords, paper dragons, and illiterate peasant armies driven into battle against their will.

More recently, American observers had not been impressed by the performance of the Chinese Nationalist troops of Generalissimo Chiang Kai-shek against the Japanese in the

Second World War. General Joseph Stilwell, the American chief of staff to Chiang during that period, frankly despised him for his military passivity and referred to him as the "Peanut." Stilwell tried in vain to reform the inefficient and corrupt Chinese Nationalist military system. In this system recruitment was done by press-gang. Many recruits were delivered to their camps with their hands and feet bound by ropes so they couldn't run away.

Stilwell despaired as he saw "officers getting rich, men dying of malnutrition, malaria, dysentery, cholera, the sick simply turned loose. Ammo and weapons being sold. Open traffic with the enemy on all 'fronts.' " During thirty-two months in China, Stilwell was never able to get the Chinese Nationalists to do any effective fighting against the Japanese.

During the Chinese civil war of 1946–1949, the Nationalists took little offensive action. Major General David Barr, U.S. military adviser to Chiang in 1948, felt that the Generalissimo's high command was politically influenced and "militarily inept." A previous American adviser, Lieutenant General Albert Wedemeyer, thought that there were "entirely too many generals in the Chinese Army, most of whom were not fitted for command in modern combat."

However, Stilwell, Barr, and Wedemeyer were referring to the Chinese Nationalists, who received a great deal of American advice and equipment. The Communists who defeated the Nationalists in the civil war were more of an enigma, since very few Westerners were able to observe them at first hand. But those few who did were favorably impressed.

Colonel Evans Carlson of the U.S. Marine Corps was the first foreign military observer to gain access to areas of north China held by the Communists. In 1937 and 1938, Carlson traveled on foot with them for more than two thousand miles. He was impressed by the toughness, mobility, and uncomplaining endurance of these Chinese soldiers. Carlson once observed a march of fifty-eight miles in thirty-two hours in mountainous country.

It was this new breed of Chinese soldier, unfamiliar to

Westerners, who entered North Korea. He was commanded
by Marshal P'eng Teh-huai, who retained his headquarters
in Mukden, Manchuria. P'eng had run away from his step-
mother's home at an early age, joined the army, and became
a platoon commander at eighteen. In 1928, at the age of
twenty-five, he led a peasant uprising in his native Hunan
province. Now forty-seven, P'eng was also a veteran of responsible commands in the anti-Japanese war and the civil
war.

Unlike the semiliterate peasant they commanded, P'eng and
his staff officers had absorbed all of Mao Tse-tung's writings
on how to deal with the Japanese invaders of China. They
were prepared to employ the same strategy in dealing with
the U.N. Command driving toward the Manchurian border.
In 1938, Mao had written, in *On Protracted War:*

> Our strategy should be to employ our main forces in mobile
> warfare over an extended, shifting, and indefinite front, a
> strategy depending for success on a high degree of mobility
> in difficult terrain, and featured by the swift attack and with-
> drawal, swift concentration and dispersal. It will be a large-
> scale war of movement rather than a positional war depending
> exclusively on defensive works with deep trenches, high for-
> tresses, and successive defensive positions. . . . We must avoid
> great decisive battles in the early stages of the war, and must
> first employ mobile warfare gradually to break the morale, the
> fighting spirit, and the military efficiency of the living forces of
> the enemy.

Chairman Mao was also a lifelong student of the philos-
opher Sun Tzu, who had written in his classic *Art of War* 3776
years before the founding of the United States: "He who is
prudent and lies in wait for an enemy who is not, will be
victorious."

P'eng and his officers now prudently lay in wait for the
enemy, employing that other key strategic concept of Chairman Mao—"luring deep." The Chinese soldiers waited, too,
eating cabbage soup and rice with noodles, cleaning and oil-
ing their Japanese and American rifles.

By October 24, the day that an optimistic General Mac-Arthur ordered all of his commanders to drive forward with "all speed" toward the Manchurian border, at least 180,000 Chinese soldiers had already crossed that border into North Korea. General MacArthur knew nothing of this vast movement. Neither, of course, did his field commanders.

CHAPTER
FIVE

"Everything Is Going Just Fine"

On October 25, Lieutenant General Walton Walker told correspondents in Pyongyang, headquarters of his 8th Army: "Everything is going just fine." General Walker had commanded the 8th Army since July 13 and had stopped its retreat of those dark days.

"Johnnie" Walker was a man of short, powerful build and was known for his bulldoglike tenacity. He carried an elephant gun with him as protection against ambush. A West Point graduate, he had won a battlefield promotion as commander of a machine-gun company in the First World War. In the early 1930's he commanded the 15th Infantry in China.

During the Second World War, Walker was one of George Patton's corps commanders. Once Patton saw him striding past his window and called out: "Walker, are you the toughest goddam soldier in this goddam army?" Without breaking stride, Walker answered: "You're goddam right."

As Walker's 8th Army moved up Korea's west coast, X

Corps,* commanded by Major General Edward Almond, advanced up Korea's east coast in accordance with General MacArthur's overall strategy. Trim and graying, "Ned" Almond was a 1915 graduate of Virginia Military Institute. He was wounded by shrapnel in the Aisne-Marne offensive of the First World War. In the Second World War, he commanded the 92nd Infantry Division, a Negro unit, on the Italian front.

Almond was assigned to MacArthur's Tokyo headquarters in 1946. Since 1949, Almond had served as chief of staff to the Supreme Commander, whom he ranked as the outstanding military genius of the twentieth century. Almond declined to extend his classification further back than that because, as he once commented, "It's hard to compare the present day with the time of Napoleon, Caesar, or Hannibal."

Almond had commanded the landing forces at the Inchon triumph. He was a member of MacArthur's inner circle. Walker was not. Walker had assumed that MacArthur would place X Corps under the 8th Army for the final drive to the Manchurian border. Instead the United Nations Commander set up X Corps as a separate command reporting directly to him through Ned Almond.

There was now a seventy-five-mile gap and little direct communication between the 8th Army and X Corps. In the middle of the gap, the Taebaek Range, some of whose mountains rose to more than seven thousand feet, formed a no-man's-land that could prevent one command from coming to to the aid of the other. And the reliance of both on motorized transport left individual units strung out over narrow, long roads that were often nothing more than wagon trails.

In establishing a divided command, MacArthur reasoned that an advance on two separate axes was the only way to solve the geographic problem posed by the rugged spinal

* The 8th Army was composed of the U.S. 2nd, 24th, and 25th Infantry Divisions; the British 27th Commonwealth Brigade; a Turkish brigade; various ROK [Republic of Korea] divisions, with the U.S. 1st Cavalry Division in reserve. X Corps consisted of the U.S. 7th Infantry Division, the U.S. 1st Marine Division, and various ROK divisions.

mountain range that lay between the west and east coasts of North Korea. However, this arrangement disturbed those in the Pentagon who followed it, for it violated the basic U.S. Army doctrine of unity of command. Lieutenant General Matthew Ridgway, Deputy Chief of Staff for Operations and Administration, was puzzled by MacArthur's "insistence on hanging on to X Corps." The Chairman of the Joint Chiefs of Staff, General Omar Bradley, was worried by the vulnerable right flank of the 8th Army and its isolation from X Corps.

On their giant war maps, the Joint Chiefs could see a situation developing where a determined attacker, even though of fewer numbers and firepower, could concentrate on isolated United Nations units with disastrous results. But nobody did anything to correct the situation; neither Walker nor Almond in the field, nor the Joint Chiefs in the Pentagon. The Army Chief of Staff, J. Lawton Collins, thought that MacArthur's battle dispositions were "the prerogative of a commander."

On the morning of October 25, the day that General Walker said that "Everything is going just fine," one South Korean battalion was only fifty miles from the Yalu and advancing swiftly on the river. But eight miles west of the crossroads hamlet of Onjong, its leading vehicles were blown apart by land mines.

The South Koreans who followed saw the leading vehicles wrecked and burning. They scrambled out of their own trucks to engage what they thought would be a small band of surviving North Koreans. But murderous machine-gun and rifle fire from high ground on both sides of the road soon destroyed the South Koreans as an organized force. In retreating to the regimental position at Onjong, they captured two prisoners. Both were Chinese.

The first snow of winter began to fall on the same cold morning of October 25. And at Unsan, a strategic road junction forty-five miles below the Manchurian border, the South Korean 1st Division's swift advance was stopped by attacks that seemed more powerful than anything that remnants of the defeated North Korean Army were capable of mounting. During the battle, these South Koreans captured a Chinese soldier. He was flown to 8th Army headquarters at Pyongyang. The prisoner maintained that there were twenty thousand Chinese Communist troops north and east of Unsan.

Around three thirty on the next morning, October 26, the South Korean regiment at Onjong was jolted awake by the sudden startling sounds of bugle calls and blasts from shepherd's horns. To the shrilling of whistles, soldiers dressed in mustard-yellow quilted-cotton uniforms closed in with submachine guns, hand grenades, and rifles. The South Koreans panicked before the assault and ran off into the hills.

At dawn of the same day, well to the north of Onjong and unaware that anything unusual had happened there, one South Korean reconnaissance platoon entered the town of Chosan on the south bank of the Yalu River. It was the first United Nations unit to reach the Manchurian border.

These South Koreans saw a narrow floating footbridge connecting Chosan to Chinese Manchuria on the Yalu's north bank. They saw no Chinese or Russians in Chosan, only North Koreans fleeing across the footbridge into Manchuria. Assisted by their American adviser, Major Harry Fleming, the South Koreans carefully set up machine guns so that this foot traffic could be stopped without firing into Manchurian soil.

Then Major Fleming and the reconnaissance platoon detailed a small detachment to remain in Chosan and returned to their regiment eighteen miles to the south. Later, the regiment was stopped by a roadblock, surrounded, and virtually annihilated. Major Fleming was wounded in fifteen places, taken prisoner, and eventually died in Chinese captivity.

In its intelligence report for October 26, the 8th Army took note of these new developments. The report said that there were indications of "some further reinforcement of North

Korean units with personnel taken from the Chinese Communist forces, in order to assist in the defense of the border." But 8th Army intelligence concluded that there were "no indications of open intervention on the part of Chinese Communist Forces in Korea."

However, the next day, October 27, thirty-year-old Major General Paik Sun Yup, the commander of the ROK 1st Division, went to Unsan. He examined the bodies of the enemy dead resulting from the engagement there. General Paik saw that the corpses carried no official identification but that the names and units of some of the dead were written in ink inside the blouses of their cotton uniforms.

The writing was in Chinese, General Paik noted. He knew this because he had served with the Japanese Manchurian Army during the Second World War. Paik then identified all of the dead soldiers as Chinese. After further investigation, he estimated that his division was faced by a Chinese division of ten thousand men.

However, the following day, October 28, General Willoughby issued the Far East Command Daily Intelligence Summary in Tokyo. In part, the summary estimated that:

> From a tactical viewpoint, with victorious U.S. Divisions in full deployment, it would appear that the auspicious time for such intervention [Chinese] has long since passed; it is difficult to believe that such a move, if planned, would have been postponed to a time when remnant North Korean forces have been reduced to a low point of effectiveness.

The day after this summary was issued, October 29, South Korean troops in the X Corps sector of northeastern Korea were attacked near the Chosin Reservoir. In the battle, they captured sixteen Chinese soldiers. The South Koreans' commander, Brigadier General Kim Baik Yil, telephoned this information to General Almond.

The next day, October 30, Almond came to the scene of the battle and interviewed the sixteen captives through an interpreter. The Chinese said that they were members of an entire division that had crossed the Yalu on the night of October 16. Almond immediately radioed this news to General MacArthur. On October 31, Almond learned that the South Koreans had captured seven more Chinese. Under interrogation, the newest prisoners said that there was a second Chinese division near the Chosin Reservoir.

As October ended, forest fires raged in the mountains of North Korea. Large smoke clouds could be seen hanging or drifting in the sky. As before, the fires had been set by the Chinese to mask what were now their extensive troop movements from aerial observation. Rumors began to sweep through the ranks of those South Korean units which had not yet been attacked that they soon would be, by *Chinese*—a word that aroused feelings of panic and terror in the South Koreans.

The sudden, startling mauling of isolated South Korean units and the stopping of their swift advance gave General Walker pause. The always vulnerable right flank of his 8th Army was now in danger of being completely exposed. Walker's initial reaction to the new developments had been that the Chinese soldiers represented only token reinforcements of North Korean units. No American troops had been attacked. Now Johnnie Walker wondered if his initial reaction were right. He ordered the United States 1st Cavalry Division (dismounted) out of reserve and north to reinforce the South Koreans at Unsan.

On November 1, one regiment of the 1st Cavalry arrived at Unsan. The waiting Chinese had the tremendous advantage of knowing that the 1st Cavalry was in Unsan. Native guerrillas quickly supplied them with this information, although to learn of American battle dispositions one could read of them in American newspapers, where they were published in detail. In contrast, the unsuspecting men of the 1st Cavalry were looking forward to nothing more eventful than marching in the Victory Parade planned for Armistice Day ten days hence in Tokyo.

General MacArthur sent no change in their orders to Almond or Walker, despite the alarming information Almond had just forwarded to him. Either the Supreme Commander had fallen victim to the wishful thinking and sometimes unjustified optimism that had characterized his career or, it could be argued, he had decided to let a situation develop where a major confrontation between the United States and Communist China would be inevitable. In any case, his intelligence chief was busy evaluating what had happened in North Korea and what was likely to happen there.

In the Eighth Report of the United Nations Command in Tokyo to the United Nations Security Council at Lake Success, New York, General Willoughby did mention the capture of Chinese prisoners. But in this report covering the period October 16 to October 31, Willoughby concluded that: "There is no positive evidence that Chinese Communists units, as such, have entered Korea."

CHAPTER

SIX

Bugles in the Night

Unsan was quiet during the daylight hours of November 1. The troopers of the 8th Cavalry Regiment who took up positions there reacted with indifference or disbelief to stories that they were facing regular Chinese troops. These tales were being circulated by South Korean soldiers and their American advisers who had already been attacked.

But as soon as night fell, the skeptical and unsuspecting Americans were suddenly struck by mortar and rocket barrages. Around 7:30 P.M., they heard the weird signaling of bugles and whistles. The thirty-five hundred men of the 8th Cavalry were then hit with an infantry assault mounted by elements of two Chinese divisions numbering twenty thousand men.

As the troopers fought to beat off the attacks and the night fighting increased in tempo, General Frank Milburn, commanding general of I Corps, held a conference at Anju attended by the commanders of the 1st Cavalry and 24th Infantry Divisions and the 1st ROK Division. That afternoon, General Walker had telephoned General Milburn and warned him that the ROK II Corps to the east had been shattered and that Milburn's right flank was unprotected. Now Milburn was alarmed by the reports sent to him of the sudden and unexpected heavy attacks on American forces around Unsan. He was aware that his overextended supply lines could not support a lengthy engagement against superior forces.

At the I Corps conference, which began at 8 P.M., Milburn ordered the 1st and 2nd Battalions of the 8th Cavalry to withdraw from Unsan immediately and to take up positions about twelve miles to the south. He had already ordered the 24th Division to stop the advance of its forward units, which were only eighteen air miles from the Yalu River. For the first time since their breakout from the Pusan perimeter in September, United Nations forces now went from the attack to the defensive.

But Milburn's decision to withdraw was made too late. The Chinese had already set up a roadblock south of the 1st and 2nd Battalions. In attempting to withdraw, the Americans ran into the roadblock. Despite heavy fighting and losses in men and equipment, they could not break through it. Survivors of the attempt abandoned their tanks, jeeps, artillery, and other heavy equipment and scattered into nearby hills to make their way southward as best they could.

While this furious action took place, another American unit remained unaware that anything had gone wrong. This was the 3rd Battalion, 8th Cavalry, commanded by Major Robert Ormond. The 3rd was detailed to guard the regimental rear and was positioned three miles southwest of Unsan, near a stream called Camel's Head Bend, which joined the Nammyon and Kuryong rivers. The command post of the 3rd Battalion was in a flat plowed field.

A bridge over the Nammyon River led to the command post. Two squads guarded the bridge, which was approached by a column of some two hundred soldiers around 3:30 A.M. of November 2. Thinking that they were South Koreans, the Americans let the column cross the bridge and march up to the battalion command post.

Then a bugle sounded. From all sides, Chinese soldiers

fired rifles into the command post and tossed grenades and explosive satchel charges at vehicles. They were followed by Chinese cavalry riding Mongolian ponies.

Most of the Americans were sleeping when the attack broke. One of them, Lieutenant W. C. Hill, thought he was dreaming when he heard a bugle blowing taps and the beat of horses' hooves. Awake, he saw shadowy figures who seemed to have come out of a burst of smoke, shooting and bayoneting any American they could find.

Major Ormond and Captain Filmore McAbee, battalion operations officer, jumped out of the command post dugout to determine what had happened. Both initially thought that the battalion had come under North Korean attack.

As McAbee neared the bridge, a bullet shattered his left shoulder blade. Another knocked off his steel helmet. Separated from Ormond, bleeding, and fighting off Chinese attackers with his pistol, the captain staggered back toward the dugout. Major Veale Moriarity, battalion executive officer, saw McAbee being trailed by four uniformed figures with fur headgear, grabbed him, and threw him into the dugout.

Inside the dugout, Moriarity killed two Chinese with his pistol. Wild hand-to-hand fighting broke out. The Chinese fired at close range and threw hand grenades, but were driven out after about half an hour. Moriarity and McAbee survived the attack, but neither ever saw Major Ormond again.

Daylight of November 2 brought relief to the 3rd Battalion only when American fighter-bombers struck at the Chinese and kept them under cover for the rest of the day. Meanwhile, other units of the 1st Cavalry Division to the south tried to break through the Chinese lines and rescue the 3rd Battalion. But they were stopped after heavy losses at a ridge near the Turtle Head Bend of the Kuryong River, which the cavalrymen dubbed "Bugle Hill."

At dusk of November 2, Major General Hobart Gay, commander of the 1st Cavalry Division, ordered the rescue units to withdraw. He remembered this as the hardest decision he ever made. It meant abandoning the 3rd Battalion to its fate.

A light plane dropped a message to the battalion, ordering it to break out of the trap in which it found itself as best it could. But the troopers decided to hang on through the night of November 2, during which they were first subjected to a mortar barrage and then to infantry attack.

The Americans set fire to their vehicles so that they could easily see and target successive waves of Chinese advancing on them across an open field. Six times, units of about four hundred men attacked the troopers. Each time the Chinese were beaten back from the main defense perimeter, but some of them overran a dugout sheltering fifty to sixty badly wounded Americans. The Chinese removed fifteen of the walking wounded, including Captain McAbee, who crawled over Chinese dead piled three high at the edge of the defense perimeter.

The 3rd Battalion held off its attackers through the day and night of November 3, but was almost out of ammunition by daylight of November 4. Those Americans who were still able to walk and fight, about two hundred men, attempted to escape south that night. They left the wounded, some two hundred and fifty men, with the battalion surgeon, Captain Clarence Anderson, who surrendered them to the Chinese.

Most members of the escape group were either killed or captured. By the afternoon of November 6, the 3rd Battalion, 8th Cavalry Regiment, had ceased to exist as an organized force.

There were other sudden developments in the far north of Korea to disquiet the United Nations Command. Until October 31, the United States Fifth Air Force had enjoyed complete dominance of the air. But then jets with swept-back wings and a speed of six hundred miles an hour crossed the Yalu River from Manchurian bases for the first time.

The jets were Soviet MIG-15's. Did their appearance mark the entry of the Russians into the war? It did not seem so, for after attacking American planes the MIG's sped back across the river into Manchuria, where the American pilots were under orders not to pursue them. At the time, it was not known whether the MIG pilots were Russian, Chinese, or North Korean. Later developments indicated that a few of the better pilots were Russian "volunteers" in the fledgling Chinese Air Force. They were dubbed *honchos*—Japanese for "boss" or "first class"—by their American opponents. Most of the rest were Chinese or North Korean. They had only recently completed training by the Russians and were not up to the expertise of the Americans, many of whom were veteran combat fliers of World War II. Although the unsettling possibility now existed that the *honchos* could reappear at any time in full force, the ability of fighter planes or bombers to play a decisive role in the kind of old-fashioned ground war that the Chinese were prepared to fight would come to disappoint the proponents of air power.

Meanwhile, to the east of Unsan, the 7th and 8th South Korean Divisions were hit with such fury by infantry attacks that they disintegrated by November 1. This debacle left General Walker with the right flank of his 8th Army completely exposed. Johnnie Walker was a hunter who had tracked big game in the Gobi Desert of Mongolia. However, the pursuit of the North Koreans fleeing toward the Yalu reminded the General more of the days when he shot quail in his native Bell County, Texas.

To Walker, this quail shoot now appeared to be over. He decided to stop the swift but uncoordinated advance of the 8th Army. The General planned to consolidate its units astride the Chongchon River prior to resuming a more orderly advance supported by an adequate supply system. The wide but shallow river slanted toward the Yellow Sea in a southwesterly direction some seventy miles below the Yalu. The Chongchon was the final major water obstacle in the western part of North Korea to reaching the Manchurian border. Control of the river's valleys and tributaries had always been considered essential by foreign invaders of Manchuria.

Walker ordered the U.S. 24th Infantry Division and the 27th British Commonwealth Brigade * to withdraw back to the Chongchon line. The order surprised the Commonwealth Brigade's commander, Brigadier Basil Coad. He knew nothing of what had happened around Unsan and thought that U.N. forces had "cracked the nut" and that the show was over.

The Commonwealth Brigade of some five thousand men was repositioned just north of the Chongchon with the mission of protecting its bridges and tank fords. This bridgehead area must be held if the U.N. offensive were to be resumed successfully. The 19th Regiment of the 24th Infantry Division was also stationed north of the river to protect crossing points. Between the Commonwealth Brigade to the west and the 19th Regiment to the east there existed a gap of five miles through which a determined attacker could move.

Scattered but violent minor engagements broke out as the Chinese first attempted, without success, to infiltrate around the river and cut off the rear of those 8th Army units stationed below it. The Commonwealth Brigade holding the bridgehead enjoyed relative quiet until dawn broke on November 5.

Then, the 61st Field Artillery Battalion of the 1st Cavalry Division was suddenly hit with a mortar barrage. This American battalion was supporting the Commonwealth Brigade. Captain Howard Moore, a battery commander, saw figures running at him through rice paddies and turned a 105-mm. howitzer on them. Other battery commanders directed the point-blank firing of artillery and automatic weapons at the attackers, who came within thirty yards of their positions before being mowed down.

Learning of the sudden assault on the American artillerymen, units of the Commonwealth Brigade hurried to their rescue. Brigadier Coad saw dead Chinese lying near the

---

* The 27th British Commonwealth Brigade was composed of the 1st Battalion of the Middlesex Regiment, the 1st Battalion of the Argyll and Sutherland Highland Regiment, and the 3rd Battalion of the Royal Australian Regiment.

Americans' gun shields and thought that the Americans had fought magnificently.

Despite air attacks, and bayonet charges by Australian members of the brigade, the Chinese kept coming through the day and into the night. The Commonwealth Brigade was forced to retreat to the Chongchon's banks, where it was separated from the American 19th Infantry Regiment by five miles of mountainous no-man's-land. The Americans were not attacked at their bridgehead position four miles above the Chongchon through the daylight hours of November 5.

As soon as night fell, Chinese soldiers padded silently on the crepe-rubber soles of their canvas shoes up Hill 123. Following telephone wires, they surprised E Company of the 2nd Battalion of the 19th Regiment, which held the extreme left flank of the regimental position. Coming upon the American soldiers from the rear as most of them slept, the Chinese killed them in their sleeping bags in the dark, shooting many in the back of the head.

Corporal Mitchell Red Cloud of E Company, however, was awake when the Chinese charged him from a brush-covered area. Firing his Browning Automatic Rifle point-blank at the Chinese one hundred feet away, Red Cloud himself was shot and knocked down. Wrapping his arm around a tree, he resumed firing until he was killed. A string of Chinese dead were later found in front of his corpse.

Private First Class Joseph Balboni of E Company was also charged by the Chinese, who crept to within seventy-five feet of him before he noticed them. Standing his ground, Balboni fired his BAR until he, too, was killed. Seventeen dead Chinese were later found near his body.

On Hill 123, the Chinese narrowly missed overrunning the 2nd Battalion position. Elsewhere, they kept up a furious assault against other battalions of the 19th Regiment throughout the night. The bridgehead was seriously threatened, but it was held.

At dawn of November 6, U.N. troops again heard

bugle notes being sounded. They braced for another violent onslaught.

It never came. In the entire 19th Regiment area, the Chinese broke off contact. The same thing happened in the Commonwealth Brigade zone. Australians in the most advanced positions saw the enemy retreating northward, as did aerial observers. This time the bugles had sounded a withdrawal rather than an attack. General Walker was left with an intact bridgehead, but also a number of baffling questions.

What did the sudden Chinese attack and equally sudden withdrawal mean? Were they in North Korea to stay, or had they simply made a token gesture of resistance and withdrawn permanently after suffering severe losses? Was the Chinese attack a diversion to mask the entry of Russian ground forces? Most importantly, in the light of these unexpected developments, what should the 8th Army do next?

General Walker was certain of one thing at least. He no longer had any doubt that the Chinese had intervened in force. On November 6, Walker cabled an irritated General MacArthur. The United Nations Commander wanted an explanation for the delay in the 8th Army's advance.

"An ambush and surprise attack by fresh, well-organized and well-trained units," Walker explained, "some of which were Chinese Communist Forces, began a sequence of events leading to a complete collapse and disintegration of ROK II Corps of three divisions. Contributing factors were intense, psychological fear of Chinese intervention and previous complacency and over-confidence in all ROK ranks. . . ."

But despite what had happened to the South Koreans and the American and British Commonwealth units as well, General Walker was still determined to drive on to the Yalu River. In the same message to General MacArthur, he wrote of "a regrouping of forces, an active defense, a build-up of supplies pending resumption of offensive and advance to the border. . . . Plans have been made for resumption of the offensive employing all forces available to the Army to meet the new factor of organized Chinese Communist Forces."

General MacArthur's impatience was satisfied by this explanation. He did not challenge Walker again. The United Nations Commander was still determined to secure all of Korea up to the Manchurian border. In pursuing his overall strategy, General MacArthur did not appear to be daunted by what had happened to Walker's command or by the parallel developments that occurred in the X Corps zone far to the east of the 8th Army.

X Corps, separated from the support of the 8th Army by a mountainous, trackless gap often as wide as seventy-five miles, was conducting an independent campaign, for all practical purposes. Ned Almond, X Corps commander, sent the ROK Capital Division, the best in the South Korean Army, up a fairly good coastal road. This led to the extreme northeast corner of Korea, bordering on Soviet Siberia. Some forty miles to the west of the South Koreans, the U.S. 7th Infantry Division was dispatched up a steep, narrow, winding road leading to the Manchurian border. While the 8th Army was being ambushed in the west, the two divisions advanced against token opposition.

The 1st Marine Division of some twenty-six thousand men was assigned to climb a miserable inland road leading from the port city of Hungnam to Yudam-ni on the western tip of the Chosin Reservoir. This reservoir provided a major source of hydroelectric power to Manchuria. After completing their march of eighty miles to the reservoir, the Marines were to move on to the Yalu River in a direction dictated by the developing tactical situation.

On November 1, the Marine Division began its journey from the port of Hungnam. Its commanding general, the tall, white-haired Oliver Smith, was aware that his Marines might encounter Chinese troops. For Smith knew that South Korean units that had already reached the Chosin Reservoir had been attacked on October 29 and had identified sixteen of their attackers as Chinese. General Smith read the 1st Marine Division's intelligence section's analysis of this event:

The capture by the 26th ROK Regt. of 16 POW's identified as being members of the 124th CCF [Chinese Communist Forces] Division would seem to indicate that the CCF has decided to intervene in the Korean War. It would indicate, also, that this reinforcement is being effected by unit rather than by piecemeal replacement from volunteer cadres. However, until more definite information is obtained it must be presumed that the CCF has not yet decided on full scale intervention. . . . The advantage to be gained by all-out intervention, at a time when the NK [North Korean] forces are on the verge of complete collapse, is not readily apparent.

This conclusion of the Marine intelligence section bore a remarkable similarity to the conclusion reached by General MacArthur's intelligence chief on October 28. On that date, General Willoughby had reported that: ". . . it is difficult to believe that such a move, if planned [Chinese intervention] would have been postponed to a time when remnant North Korean forces have been reduced to a low point of effectiveness."

Whatever his private misgivings might have been, General Smith followed the orders of General Almond, who was in turn following the desires of General MacArthur, and sent the 1st Marine Division north toward the Chosin Reservoir over the road known officially as the MSR—the Main Supply Route. In reality, it was the only supply route.

"We are scattered all over the landscape," Ned Almond observed of his X Corps command as it pushed north. Leading the 1st Marine Division was its 7th Regiment, commanded by Colonel Homer Litzenberg. He was stocky and square-faced, a product of the Pennsylvania steel country who had risen through the ranks and fought in both Europe and the Pacific in the Second World War.

Litzenberg was convinced that his 7th Regiment would come up against the Chinese. In an informal talk to his officers and noncommissioned officers before the regiment left Hungnam, he told them that they soon might be fighting the first battle of the Third World War.

"We can expect to meet Chinese Communist troops,"

Litzenberg concluded his informal talk, "and it is important that we win the first battle. The results of that action will reverberate around the world, and we want to make sure that the outcome has an adverse effect in Moscow as well as Peking."

The 7th Marine Regiment encountered only sporadic resistance during the first thirty miles of its journey toward the Chosin Reservoir. Most of the Marines rode in trucks over the fairly level dirt and gravel Main Supply Route to the village of Sudong, which they reached at dusk of November 2. The Marines then bivouacked and tried to get some sleep. The next morning they were to begin the difficult part of their journey on foot, for north of Sudong the Main Supply Route changed to a thin cart trail leading to mile-high mountain peaks.

The Marines' rest was disturbed around 11 P.M. when colored flares exploded over their positions. Bugle calls were then heard. Infantry began smashing at the Marines with a well-coordinated double envelopment. Dawn of November 3 revealed that the 1st and 2nd Battalions were cut off from the rest of the 7th Regiment. "We found that we were in a dickens of a mess," Major Webb Sawyer, commander of the 2nd Battalion, later reported.

However, the superior firepower of the Marines and the calling in of air support from the 1st Marine Air Wing, which dropped rockets and napalm bombs trailing orange flames, relieved the two battalions. The night of November 3 was relatively calm. As day broke on November 4, Colonel Litzenberg was determined to advance, but he now wanted to gain a clearer picture of what his regiment might be coming up against.

What the thirty-five hundred men of the 7th Regiment were coming up against, as the patrols and interrogations of prisoners indicated, was ten thousand men of the 124th Division of the Chinese People's Liberation Army. At the time, the Marines did not learn that two more divisions of the PLA were also lying in wait for them.

Somewhat more warily now, Litzenberg sent the 7th Regiment forward. Chinese resistance was light during the day and night of November 4, but it turned savage when day broke on November 5. But again the superior firepower of the Marine air, artillery, and mortars prevented the Chinese from blocking the road to the reservoir.

The night of November 5 was relatively calm, as were the daylight hours of the sixth. By dusk of the sixth, the Marines had advanced some six miles from Sudong through the mountain hamlet of Chinghung-ni and begun the steep ascent to Koto-ri. Eight of the ten miles of this journey twisted through the Funchilin Pass, where there was a chasm on one side and a cliff on the other. The Chinese were positioned at the top of the pass with the Marines below them directly under their guns. But dawn of November 7 in the northeast brought with it the same mysterious development that had taken place to the northwest. The Chinese did not open fire, broke off contact, and vanished.

The Marines continued on through Funchilin Pass, for despite the clear evidence of Chinese intervention no changes in their orders were sent to Almond of X Corps or Walker of the 8th Army. It was not, of course, the responsibility of these field commanders to decide whether or not the drive to the Yalu River should be continued in light of the sudden Chinese attacks and equally sudden mysterious withdrawals. This responsibility rested first with Douglas MacArthur in Tokyo, but above him with the Joint Chiefs of Staff in Washington, and ultimately, because military leadership is thrust upon the President by the Constitution, with Harry Truman.

CHAPTER
SEVEN

The President

Korea was only one of Harry Truman's problems as November of 1950 began. In directing the foreign policy of the United States he held to the position that the main menace to the Western world was the Soviet threat to Europe. The war in Korea was being waged for limited objectives and with the desire to avoid wrapping the world in the flames of a general conflict.

In Washington, military experts were working on a blueprint for the North Atlantic Treaty Organization to counter the Soviet threat. Measures to be taken if western Europe were invaded within the next six months were being seriously considered.

Another problem was Indochina, where a French Army of 150,000 men had been unable to suppress Ho Chi Minh's Viet Minh rebel Communist army. The President learned that the French allies of the United States had just been forced to retreat from their strong points along the Chinese border. Lang Son, a fortress frequently regarded as the key to Hanoi itself, was abandoned. The French were demanding a greater American involvement in Indochina. "They blackmailed us," said Dean Acheson. "At every meeting when we asked for greater effort in Europe they brought up Indochina and later Africa."

The President knew that, five years after World War II, the United States did not have the military power to provide a shield for western Europe in addition to undertaking a major commitment in Korea, Indochina, or China. Defense budgets had been cut to the point where the United States Army was split up into ten understrength divisions armed principally with World War II weapons. The Army's 592,000 men were less than half the number it had had on Pearl Harbor Day. The Navy had been reduced in strength as drastically as the Army. Although the Air Force remained strong and the United States possessed the atom bomb, the Soviet Union now had the bomb, too.

It was in the light of these worldwide problems that the President had to consider the Korean situation. On the domestic political front, the action he had taken in an unfamiliar Asiatic country was not popular with, or completely understood by, most voters. Congress had issued no formal declaration of war. The leader of the Senate Republicans, Robert Taft of Ohio, complained that the President had "usurped the power of Congress" by sending American combat troops into Korea.

At a press conference back on June 29, Truman had not helped to clarify the situation when he told reporters that "We are not at war" and agreed that it was correct to describe what was taking place in Korea as a "police action under the United Nations." Nevertheless, none of the President's advisers had given him any firm warning by the beginning of November that this police action was not coming to a favorable conclusion and contained the explosive potential of starting World War III. Therefore, as was his usual custom, he planned to go to Independence, Missouri, on November 7 to cast his ballot in the congressional elections.

However, an event took place in Washington on the quiet, unseasonably warm afternoon of November 1 that would have changed that plan if its purpose had succeeded. The President was napping in historic Blair House, where he lived while the White House was being renovated, when he was awakened by the sound of gunfire. He went to the window of his upstairs bedroom in his underwear, peered down, and saw a dead man lying in the sunlight on the entrance steps. Blood flowed from the man's riddled chest and stained his blue-green pinstriped suit and blue shirt.

The dead man turned out to be Griselio Torresola, a Puerto Rican armed with a German P-38 automatic pistol. Lying near him, still alive but severely wounded by guards, two of whom had themselves been shot in the fray, was another Puerto Rican, Oscar Collazo, who was holding a Luger. Both Torresola and Collazo had failed to shoot their way into Blair House in a plot by Puerto Rican nationalist fanatics to murder the President.

Truman took the thwarted assassination attempt philo-sophically as being part of the burden of the Presidency. To a military adviser, Admiral William Leahy, he remarked: "The only thing you have to worry about is bad luck. I never have bad luck." The President was now nearing the midpoint of his first full term, having taken the oath of office on April 12, 1944, after the death of Franklin Roosevelt. Truman had served as Vice-President for only eighty-two days when Roose-velt died, and the latter had not taken much time to instruct him in all of the complex problems with which a new President would be faced.

As a candidate, Vice-President-elect, and Vice-President, Truman saw Roosevelt only eight times in the entire year before Roosevelt's death. But Truman stepped in and guided the world's most powerful nation through the end of World War II and a postwar era in which, according to Dean Ache-son, "the whole world structure and order that we had in-herited from the nineteenth century was gone."

Truman's decision to intervene in Korea, a little piece of Asiatic peninsula about which few Americans could pass any kind of quiz, was quick and courageous. He was sometimes impetuous, but he was also unwavering in his determination to act when he thought he was right. On his desk rested a small, hand-lettered sign of which he was very fond. The sign read: THE BUCK STOPS HERE.

The Cold War was at its height during Truman's presidency. He met what he saw as the danger posed by Russian Communist expansionism with bold and imaginative countermeasures—aid to Greece and Turkey under the Truman Doctrine, the European Recovery Program, the Berlin airlift, NATO, the Marshall Plan. Compared to these successes in Europe, Truman's attempt to shore up the Chiang Kai-shek regime in China with financial and military aid was a failure. But there undoubtedly never was an American solution for this complex, intractable Chinese problem.

With United States intervention in Korea, the nation was once more confronting communism in Asia. This time the venture seemed to be turning out well. "Harry's the luckiest buzzard I ever knew," Eddie Jacobson, his onetime partner in a Kansas City haberdashery shop, remarked after Truman became President, "but I'll give him this: he's got plenty of guts."

Truman needed guts to survive and push forward on the often discouraging road he had traveled to his second term as President. Reared on a farm near Independence, Missouri, his early ventures into farming, zinc mining, and oil speculation were failures. The haberdashery shop he opened in the fall of 1919 went bankrupt in 1922. Truman then turned to politics and in 1922 was elected county judge of Jackson County, Missouri, largely because of the support of his fellow veterans in the Missouri National Guard.

Truman was defeated for reelection in 1925 and found himself unemployed and in debt at the age of forty, with a wife and a year-old daughter. He studied law part-time for three years at Kansas City Law School, although he did not graduate, and also sold auto club memberships, organized a building and loan company, and with some partners bought control of a small bank, which failed.

Truman's return to politics was made possible when Tom Pendergast, the powerful Democratic boss of Kansas City, supported his election as presiding judge of the county court of Jackson County. Truman held this office from 1927 to 1934, when he was elected United States Senator with the backing of the Pendergast machine. He won reelection as a Senator in 1940, although President Roosevelt was one of many who doubted that he could do it. In 1944, Truman was chosen by the Democratic Convention as Roosevelt's running mate, not because he was especially favored by the President but because he was acceptable to New Dealers and powerful labor leaders as well as conservative Democrats in farm states.

Harry Truman ran for the presidency on his own in 1948 against a formidable opponent, the former college baritone at the University of Michigan, crusading district attorney, and crisply efficient Governor of the most populous state, New York, Thomas E. Dewey. The voters seemed weary of the frenetic years of New Deal innovation and postwar adjustment and in a mood for tranquillity. Truman was the definite underdog. Newspapers were for Dewey eight to one in terms of their circulation. Public opinion polls strongly favored the Governor of New York. The leading poll, conducted by Elmo Roper, concluded on August 29 that a Dewey victory was so obvious that further polls would hardly be worth the effort.

Dewey, sensing victory, ran a somnolent campaign designed to avoid controversy. He also projected a somewhat waxen image that earned him the sobriquet of "the bridegroom on the wedding cake." Truman undertook a vigorous whistle-stop campaign, in which he traveled 30,000 miles and gave 351 speeches before more than 12 million people. In these speeches of the "Give 'em hell, Harry" variety, the President castigated the Republican-controlled 80th Congress as a "do-nothing" Congress responsible for most of the nation's ills. Truman surprised the newspapers and the pollsters by defeating Dewey.

Although the American effort to resist Communist expansion in Europe was continued, the North Korean attack upon South Korea presented the Truman Administration with a test of its determination to stand firm against communism in Asia. The President did not hesitate to send in American troops under the flag of the United Nations. This undertaking, under the military direction of General MacArthur, now appeared to have been successful. As *Time* magazine put it in its issue of October 30: "Now that the war was ending the U.N. liberators of Korea faced two big problems—economic reconstruction and political reconstruction."

Truman's relations with MacArthur also appeared to be satisfactory as a result of the Wake Island Conference and the coming triumph. Unknown to the public, their relations had not always been satisfactory. Back on August 26, MacArthur had issued a message to the annual encampment of the Veterans of Foreign Wars. He did so without giving prior notification to the President, the State and Defense Departments, or the Joint Chiefs of Staff.

The General's message described what was, to the State Department, a new foreign policy for the whole of the Pacific. MacArthur decried as "appeasement" the "fallacious and threadbare argument" that to encourage Chiang Kai-chek would "alienate continental Asia." Since the message collided with the official Administration policy of discouraging Chiang from attacking the Chinese mainland, Truman ordered MacArthur to withdraw it. The angered President also thought seriously of relieving the General as military commander in the Far East and leaving him only in charge of the Japanese occupation. But Truman decided against this step, and the ill feelings engendered by MacArthur's challenge to presidential authority were soon erased by the Inchon triumph and the General's victorious drive into North Korea.

Nevertheless, President Truman was concerned enough about the first reports of the capture of Chinese prisoners to ask the Joint Chiefs to obtain from MacArthur an estimate of the situation. MacArthur's reply, received in Washington on November 4, was of a calming nature. "It is impossible at this time to authoritatively appraise the actualities of Chinese Communist intervention in North Korea," the General reported. He then went on to appraise the battle intelligence coming to him from the front and concluded: "I recommend against hasty conclusions which might be premature and believe that a final appraisement should await a more complete accumulation of military facts."

To President Truman, this message discounted the possibility that the Chinese intervention signified a "new war." He left Washington on the afternoon of November 4 and went to St. Louis, where that night he gave a fighting speech at the Kiel Auditorium in which he denounced the Republican Party as the captive of "special interests" determined to kill the New Deal and his own Fair Deal. The next day he traveled to Kansas City, Missouri, and he was in that city on November 6 preparing to go on to Independence to cast his ballot on November 7 when General MacArthur issued a public communiqué from his headquarters in Tokyo.

The Korean War had been brought to a practical end by the defeat of the North Koreans, the United Nations Commander informed the world on November 6. However, in the face of this victory, he reported: "The Communists committed one of the most offensive acts of international lawlessness of historic record by moving, without notice of belligerence, elements of alien Communist forces across the Yalu River into North Korea and massing a great concentration of possible reinforcing divisions with adequate supply behind the privileged sanctuary of the adjacent Manchurian border. . . ."

This communiqué came as "something of a shock" to President Truman. It took such a different tack from MacArthur's calming report of only two days before that Dean Acheson characterized the General's reports beginning at this time as "schizophrenic."

In addition to issuing his public communiqué, General MacArthur made a private decision to stop what he now regarded as "massive Chinese intervention." He ordered Lieutenant General George Stratemeyer, commander of the U.S. Far East Air Force, to send the next day, November 7, ninety

B-29 bombers to destroy the important bridge over the Yalu linking Antung in Manchuria to Sinuiju in North Korea.

MacArthur felt that the B-29's were the only weapon he had to cut the lines of supply and communication between Manchuria and North Korea. Of course, it was not known yet that over two hundred thousand Chinese had already crossed the Yalu bridges. But it was known that convoys were crossing the river. Marine Corps pilots reported the southward bound traffic to their intelligence officers variously as "heavy," "very heavy," and "tremendous."

Before going to bed on November 6, MacArthur informed the Joint Chiefs of his bombing order. This information was received with consternation by the Pentagon and the State Department, which had a policy of not permitting bombing within five miles of the Yalu in order to avoid provoking the Chinese. Navigational errors could also lead to difficulties with the Russians.

Opinions on the bombing order were exchanged by officials of the Defense and State Departments. Undersecretary of Defense Robert Lovett felt that the risk of bombing Antung was greater than the advantages to be gained by interrupting the bridge traffic there. Assistant Secretary of State for Far Eastern Affairs Dean Rusk observed that the British had been advised that the United States would do nothing that might involve striking Manchuria without prior consultation. If Chinese territory were attacked, Rusk also noted, the Russians were obligated to come to the aid of the Chinese by a mutual assistance pact.

Dean Acheson relayed these opinions by telephone to President Truman in Kansas City. The President told Acheson that he would approve the bombing if "there was an immediate and serious threat to the security of our troops." Until this was ascertained, it could be postponed. The Joint Chiefs should ask MacArthur for his estimate of the situation and his justification for bombing along the Manchurian border.

Because of the fourteen-hour time difference between Tokyo

and Washington, MacArthur was asleep when a messenger awakened him at 2 A.M. of November 7 with an urgent cable from Secretary of Defense Marshall. MacArthur jumped out of bed and read the cable at his desk with incredulity. He was directed "to postpone all bombing within five miles of the Manchurian border" and advised that "consideration was urgently being given to the Korean situation at the Government level."

To MacArthur, this meant that protection was being extended to the Chinese to move men and supplies over the river and establish a five-mile bridgehead on the North Korean side of it. "It would be impossible to exaggerate my astonishment," he later wrote, "and I at once protested."

MacArthur's protest to the Joint Chiefs, in contrast to his unruffled views of three days before, was both vigorous and alarming: "Men and material in large force are pouring across all bridges over the Yalu from Manchuria," he cabled, in part. "This movement not only jeopardizes but threatens the ultimate destruction of the forces under my command. . . . I trust that the matter be immediately brought to the attention of the President, as I believe your instructions may well result in a calamity of major proportions for which I cannot accept the responsibility without his personal and direct understanding of the situation. . . ."

The matter was immediately brought to the attention of the President by General Bradley, who read MacArthur's message over the telephone to Truman in Kansas City. The President expressed his concern about the grave dangers inherent in bombing targets so close to Chinese and Russian soil. But, as he later wrote, ". . . since General MacArthur was on the scene and felt so strongly that this was of unusual urgency, I told Bradley to give him the 'go-ahead.' "

The Joint Chiefs then cabled MacArthur that: "The situation depicted in your message is considerably changed from that reported in last sentence of your message [of November 4] which was our last report from you." He was authorized to bomb the Korean ends of the Yalu bridges only, but not any of the dams or power plants on the river. The Joint Chiefs concluded by asking to be kept informed "of important changes in situation as they occur and that your estimate as requested in our message be submitted as soon as possible."

On November 7, General MacArthur complied with the request for his estimate. He informed Washington that his appraisal of November 4 that the Chinese had not undertaken a full-scale intervention was still correct. However, he did concede that further reinforcement of those forces that had intervened might render "our resumption of advance impossible and even forcing a movement in retrograde." But the U.N. Commander still intended to advance to take "accurate measure . . . of enemy strength."

MacArthur sent another message to the Joint Chiefs on November 7. This one referred to the Russian-built MIG-15 jet fighters, which from November 1 onward had been shooting across the border from Manchurian bases. The MIG's were attacking U.N. aircraft flying south of the Yalu and then darting back into China.

"Hostile planes are operating from bases west of the Yalu River against our forces in North Korea. These planes are appearing in increasing numbers. The distance from the Yalu to the main line of contact is so short that it is almost impossible to deal effectively with the hit and run tactics now being employed. The present restrictions imposed on my area of operation provide a complete sanctuary for hostile air immediately upon their crossing the Manchurian–North Korean border. The effect of this abnormal condition upon the morale and combat efficiency of both air and ground troops is major.

"Unless corrective measures are promptly taken this factor can assume decisive proportions. Request instructions for dealing with this new and threatening development."

While the President and his advisers in the Defense and State Departments were trying to figure out what instructions to forward, General MacArthur was chafing under his authorization to bomb only the Korean ends of the Yalu bridges. To the U.N. Commander, this was "the most indefensible and ill-conceived decision ever forced on a field commander in our nation's history." He became so frustrated by the restriction that he wrote out a dispatch asking for relief from duty in the Far East.

When he learned of this, General Doyle Hickey, MacArthur's Deputy Chief of Staff, told him that to seek relief at such a critical time might demoralize the Army. MacArthur then tore up the dispatch.

Unaware that MacArthur was thinking of being relieved from duty, Secretary of Defense Marshall at this time sent him a placating message. Marshall said that the Administration realized "your difficulty in fighting a desperate battle in a mountainous region under winter conditions." The Secretary of Defense added that he understood "the difficulty involved in conducting such a battle under necessarily limited conditions and the necessity of keeping the distant headquarters, in Washington, informed of developments and decisions. However, this appears to be unavoidable. We are faced with an extremely grave international problem."

MacArthur's reaction to this conciliatory message was to think that by meeting naked force with appeasement, military disaster would be perpetuated in Korea and communism would be enabled to make its bid for most of Asia. To him, Washington did not seem to comprehend this complex, long-range problem.

In Washington, the Secretary of State, who was the official primarily responsible for dealing with the political aspects of the problem, was finding what he considered MacArthur's mercurial temperament and moods difficult to follow. From November 4 to 9, Dean Acheson later wrote, the General "went from calm confidence, warning against hasty judgment until all the facts were in, through ringing the tocsin on the sixth to proclaim that hordes of men were pouring into

Korea and threatening to overwhelm his command, to confidence again on the ninth that he could deny the enemy reinforcement."

On November 9, MacArthur had cabled the Joint Chiefs
that with his "air power, now unrestricted so far as Korea is
concerned . . . I can deny reinforcements coming across the
Yalu in sufficient strength to prevent the destruction [sic] of
those forces now arrayed against me in North Korea."

President Truman was the final arbiter of what should be
done in Korea. He also had to answer to the United Nations.
Truman did not want the fighting in Korea to develop into a
general war. He asked the Joint Chiefs for their opinions on
the significance of the Chinese intervention. On November 8,
the Joint Chiefs informed the President that every effort should
be made to settle the problem by political means, preferably
through the United Nations. But pending "further clarification
as to the military objectives of the Chinese Communists and
the extent of their intended commitments" the missions assigned to MacArthur "should be kept under review, but should
not be changed."

Despite all that had happened, the Joint Chiefs thus advised the President that MacArthur should be allowed to follow the orders given to him on October 9. These orders read:
"In the event of the open or covert employment anywhere in
Korea of major Chinese Communist units, without prior announcement, you should continue the action as long as, in
your judgment, action by forces now under your control
offers a reasonable chance of success."

On November 9, the National Security Council met in
Washington and reviewed these recommendations without
changing MacArthur's orders. In reviewing the intentions of
the Chinese, General Bradley, speaking for the Joint Chiefs,
said that there were three possibilities.

First, the Chinese might only want to protect their interests in the hydroelectric works along the Yalu by creating a
buffer zone. Second, the Chinese might want to lure the United
States into a war of attrition. This would so involve American

forces that the United States would risk losing if the Russians chose to begin a global war. Third, the Chinese might want to drive United States forces out of Korea altogether. This last possibility could lead to World War III, as the Chinese were not strong enough to do it alone and would need Soviet assistance.

No one at the meeting, which was attended by the Secretaries of Defense and State and the Joint Chiefs of Staff, engaged in further speculation by posing a fourth alternative in the form of a question: if the roles were reversed, what would the United States do if an army hostile to its government, despite pronouncements of benign intentions, approached its borders from Mexico?

Acheson summarized the meeting, according to President Truman, by pointing out that it "was agreed that General MacArthur's directive should not now be changed and that he should be free to do what he could in a military way, but without bombing Manchuria." Acheson, who felt that all of the President's advisers realized that something was badly wrong but did not quite know what to do about it, later wrote that here the Administration "missed its last chance to halt the march to disaster in Korea."

General MacArthur, since no one had instructed him otherwise, intended to continue the advance to the Yalu River. However, he remained under the restriction to bomb only the Korean ends of the Yalu bridges. And authorization was denied to him to allow his fliers to engage in "hot pursuit" of the Russian-built MIG's across the Yalu into Manchuria. The United Nations allies of the United States objected to this as a dangerous provocation.

Through the middle of November, the reluctance of the Administration to restrain MacArthur and his own reviving optimism were undoubtedly influenced by the enigma of the Chinese withdrawal after their initial attacks. They seemed to have vanished from the earth. It was anybody's guess whether or not they would reappear.

In this guessing game, there was no real disagreement

between the U.N. Commander and his advisers in Tokyo and the generals and diplomats in Washington. The simple fact was that they were all groping in the dark. In Peking, however, the Chinese Communist leaders had decided on a course of action after reviewing the results of what they termed their First Phase Offensive.

CHAPTER
EIGHT

An Enigma

Although Chinese forces appeared to have vanished from North Korea after the first week in November, the Korean situation was far from forgotten within China itself. At this time, the Chinese Government stepped up its anti-American propaganda campaign. This had already been virulent enough, as indicated by a quotation from author Mao Tun read in English during the Radio Peking broadcast to North America on August 30:

> This mad dog [the United States] seizes Taiwan between its hind legs while with its teeth it violently bites the Korean people. Now one of its forelegs has been poked into our Northeast front. Its bloodswollen eyes cast around for something further to attack. All the world is under its threat. The American imperialist mad dog is half beaten up. Before it dies, it will go on biting and tearing.

Now the Chinese People's Committee in Defense of World Peace and Against American Aggression, formed in Peking on October 26, opened a massive propaganda campaign to mobilize the populace. Its theme was "Resist the U.S., Aid

Korea, Protect Our Homes, and Defend Our Country." All communications media hit hard at this theme, which employed the key term *k'ang yi,* or active defense. This had previously been used in fighting the Japanese and the Chinese Nationalists. Public meetings were held in every major city in China. Thousands vowed to defend China amidst the "spontaneous demands of volunteers anxious to fight the American imperialists in Korea."

On November 3, Radio Peking declared that the fighting in Korea posed a direct threat to China's safety and that the Chinese people should aid the North Koreans and resist the United States. Four days later, the official North Korean communiqué announced that "volunteer units formed by the Chinese people participated in operations along with the People's Armed Forces, under the unified command of General Headquarters . . . [and] mounted fierce counteroffensives on the west front on October 25."

On November 11, a spokesman for the Ministry of Foreign Affairs conceded that Chinese volunteers were fighting in North Korea. He denied, however, that the Chinese Government had sent them there and remarked that: "This reasonable expression of the Chinese people's will to assist Korea and resist American aggression is not without precedent in the history of the world. . . . As is well known, in the 18th century, the progressive people of France, inspired and led by Lafayette, assisted the American people in their war of independence by similar voluntary action. . . ."

While maintaining the fiction of the volunteers, the Chinese leaders were deciding what to do with the regular troops they had órdered into inactivity but kept hidden in the mountains of North Korea. Further action would depend on an evaluation of the response of the United Nations General Assembly and the United States to the First Phase Offensive.

The men making this evaluation shared many experiences that distinguished them from their civilian counterparts in any other government and shaped their view of the world. Chairman Mao Tse-tung, Premier and Foreign Minister Chou

En-lai, Commander of the Fourth Field Army Lin Piao, Chief of Staff Chu Teh, and their associates on the Central Committee and in the Politburo were veterans of twenty-eight years of battle as an armed minority before gaining power. This included fighting both the Chinese Nationalists of Chiang Kai-shek and the Japanese invaders of North China. The Japanese, who had approached North China through Korea and occupied Manchuria, were a particularly brutal foe. Their "three-all" policy, instituted by General Okamura Yasuji when he took command of the North China Area Army in July 1941, was "kill all, burn all, destroy all."

The Chinese leaders, then, were no strangers to battle and to taking risks to gain their ends. And while they were all dedicated Communists patterned on the Russian model, they were also Chinese. Chairman Mao did not actually sit on the Dragon Throne, but he lived in the golden-roofed palaces of the Chinese emperors who had once ruled their subjects and tributary peoples under the Mandate of Heaven. The traditional assumption of the innate superiority of the Middle Kingdom to the culture of the "foreign barbarians" persisted in the Chinese consciousness. Suspicion and hostility toward them were easily aroused.

To most Chinese, the "foreign devils" had been a source of nothing but trouble. Peking was occupied by European troops in 1860, and forty years later by American and European soldiers. Chinese dignity was affronted. Concessions and special privileges were extracted from weak Chinese governments by the Westerners. In 1931, the Japanese invaded and then occupied Manchuria. Now still another foreign army was approaching China's borders.

Dean Acheson and the State Department and General MacArthur and his staff appeared to be operating with almost total incomprehension of this Chinese frame of reference. The Chinese Communist leaders, new to power and international politics, did not have any better comprehension of American intentions. But then there had been no logical consistency to the actions of the United States.

In June, the stated purpose of the United States Government was to repel the North Korean aggression against the south. By August it was the destruction of the North Korean Army. By October it was to unify all of Korea. Now, in November, American planes were bombing bridges along the Manchurian border.

President Truman did not want to cross the Manchurian border and extend the war into China. But he had not found a way to make the Chinese leaders believe this. They had seen no evidence that he could restrain MacArthur, an avowed opponent of communism in any form and a man who did not keep his opinions secret. The General had described the initial Chinese entry into the Korean fighting as "an act of international lawlessness." From the Chinese point of view, their entry might be simply a legitimate response to what they considered an aggressive threat to their borders. Both sides, in the figurative as well as the literal sense of the phrases, were talking different languages.

Subsequent evidence would indicate that the Chinese Communists had very little, if anything, to do with instigating the original North Korean attack upon South Korea. North Korea was a Soviet satellite, and the Chinese Communists displayed scant interest in the affairs of their smaller neighbor. In June 1950, the new regime had only been in official existence for nine months and had plenty of domestic problems to worry about.

Droughts and pests afflicted those areas which were not drenched by the rains of the summer and fall of 1949, which broke ten-year records. The resulting crop losses caused widespread famine. Mountain bandits, non-Chinese peoples, traditional secret societies, and surviving Nationalist forces had to be "pacified." These problems existed in an underdeveloped country already crippled by foreign and civil war.

The expansionist military ambitions of the Chinese Communists centered on Tibet and Formosa (Taiwan) rather than Korea. Their designs on Formosa were frustrated by the U.S. Seventh Fleet, which shielded the island from mainland invasion. But Tibet, considered to be one of the "lost territories" of the old empire by Chairman Mao, was eventually invaded by the People's Liberation Army on October 7. This aroused the displeasure of India, which had been supporting the entry of the Chinese Communists into the United Nations. It was only when United States troops crossed the 38th Parallel and headed toward the Manchurian border after repeated warnings had gone unheeded that the Chinese Communists decided to intervene.

There were many logical reasons why otherwise reasonable men had not taken these warnings seriously. As MacArthur's intelligence chief, General Willoughby, later put it: "Was Communist China prepared to take the stunning gamble of throwing its ground forces into war against a country possessing the atom bomb and complete air control of the campaign area? Could she afford to risk the destruction of her flimsy industrial base and the severance of her tenuous supply lines from the Soviets, which would deny her the resources to support modern war or to sustain large military forces in the field and in turn so weaken the Peiping Communist government's hold in Asia as to threaten the eventuality of a Red debacle?"

General Willoughby did not think so, and neither did General MacArthur. But then neither did Dean Acheson, who thought that the Chinese had more to fear from their fellow Communists the Russians than from the United States. Acheson said and did nothing to indicate that he had changed his opinion expressed back on September 10: "Now I give the people in Peking credit for being intelligent enough to see what is happening to them. Why they should want to further their own dismemberment and destruction by getting at cross purposes with all the free nations of the world who are inherently their friends and have always been friends of the Chinese as against this imperialism coming down from the north I cannot see. . . ."

However, the Chinese Communists themselves saw the advance of the U.N. Command to the Manchurian border as a major, immediate threat. And looking at the situation from their own point of view, rather than from the rational way Western observers thought they should be looking at it, the Chinese leaders could see at least two good reasons for intervening in Korea.

First, it would be advantageous to keep a friendly Communist government in existence in North Korea. Passive acceptance of a democratic Korea united under the U.N. flag might encourage MacArthur, Chiang, and their supporters to attack China itself, where many internal weaknesses could be exploited.

Second, after centuries of isolation and domination by the West, the "sick man of Asia" could now demonstrate that it was not simply a Soviet puppet but a major force to be reckoned with in world affairs. This could be accomplished by a smashing victory over the celebrated General MacArthur. The chances for such a victory seemed favorable, as the U.N. Command continued to be lured ever deeper to where it could be engaged in a classic Maoist war of annihilation.

The enigma of the Chinese withdrawal after their initial attacks was, to the Chinese, no enigma at all. The First Phase Offensive, the cessation of which both confused and encouraged the U.N. Command, was primarily a defensive operation. It slowed the drive to the Yalu and caused U.N. forces to develop fixed positions. It gave the Chinese Government an opportunity to assess the reaction of the United Nations and the United States to Chinese intervention. Apparently, this had not caused the U.N. Command to halt its pronounced intention to drive all the way to the Yalu. Nor did it call forth an extreme punitive response, such as the atom bomb.

The Chinese Communist leaders were prepared to take the calculated risk of an atomic attack. They did not believe it would be decisive against the most populous, and largely agrarian, people on earth. In 1946, Mao Tse-tung had said to an American journalist: "The atom bomb is a paper tiger with which the U.S. reactionaries try to terrify the people. It looks terrible, but in fact it is not. Of course, the atom bomb is a weapon of mass destruction, but the outcome of war is decided by the people, not by one or two new weapons." Now a basic directive of the "Resist America, Aid Korea" propaganda campaign was to tell the Chinese people:

> The atomic bomb is now no longer monopolized by the U.S. The Soviet Union has it too. If the U.S. dares to use the atomic bombs, she naturally will get retaliation. . . . The atomic bomb itself cannot be the decisive factor in a war. . . . It cannot be employed on the battlefield to destroy directly the fighting power of the opposing army, in order not to annihilate the users themselves. It can only be used against a big and concentrated object like a big armament industry center or huge concentration of troops. Therefore, the more extensive the opponents' territory is and the more scattered the opponents' population is, the less effective will the atom bomb be.

The First Phase Offensive also gave the Chinese High Command an opportunity to test and assess U.N. military capabilities. With their own performance, the Chinese were satisfied, although their 124th Division was virtually destroyed by the U.S. 1st Marine Division in their engagement along the Main Supply Route to the Chosin Reservoir.

The headquarters of the 66th Army compiled a study entitled "Primary Conclusions of Battle Experiences at Unsan." This analyzed American strengths and weaknesses. Respect was accorded to American firepower, but American infantrymen were found to be ". . . weak, afraid to die, and haven't the courage to attack or defend." The study then formulated these principles for future Chinese action:

> As a main objective, one of the units must fight its way rapidly around the enemy and cut off their rear. . . . Route of attack must avoid highways and flat terrain in order to keep tanks and artillery from hindering the attack operations. . . . Night warfare in mountainous terrain must have a definite plan and liaison between platoon commands. Small leading patrol groups attack and then sound the bugle. A large number will at that time follow in column.

In summarizing the results of the First Phase Offensive, the study concluded: "At that time, we did not fully comprehend the tactical characteristics and combat strength of the enemy, and we lacked experience in mountain warfare. Moreover, we engaged the enemy (first, in the form of interdiction, then in that of attack) without sufficient preparation; yet the result was satisfactory."

The breaking off of the First Phase Offensive, so puzzling to Western observers, was simply an occasion for the Chinese high command to rest and reorganize its forces and to bring in more from Manchuria. As to what the Chinese were going to do next, not all American intelligence sources were groping in the dark. At least one was chillingly correct. Karl Lott Rankin, the American Ambassador to Nationalist China, sent the following cable to the Department of State from Taiwan on November 6:

> Chinese military intelligence forwarded to Washington by the Embassy's service attachés during the past few days lends strong support to the assumption that the Chinese communists plan to throw the book at the United Nations forces in Korea and in addition to step up their pressure in Indochina. Allowance evidently should be made for wishful thinking among the Chinese military, most of whom regard a general conflict as the only means of liberating China from the communists. In the present instance, however, such a caveat still leaves an imposing array of apparently established facts, as well as evidence of sincerity among the best informed Chinese, such as to render quite possible the correctness of their consensus of opinion that all-out action in Korea by the Chinese communists should be expected.
>
> The reasons why the Chinese communists have so far delayed their entry into Korea in force, quite aside from any speculation on influences exerted by Moscow, may include:
> 1. The Chinese communists had assumed that the North Koreans would win; hence they had not prepared to intervene earlier.
> 2. Postponing any major effort on their part until the fighting reached the region of the Korean-Manchurian frontier served

to shorten their lines of communication—a particularly important point in view of the fact that United Nations forces control sea and air—and also gave them the maximum time for preparation. In addition to bringing up forces from other parts of China, it was necessary to replenish stocks of equipment and supplies in Manchuria which had been seriously depleted in extending aid to the North Koreans.

3. In the above-mentioned frontier area full advantage can be taken of the degree to which world opinion has been conditioned to acts of aggression and now looks upon a few regiments being identified on the wrong side of the border as indicating rather less than overt action. Meantime the United Nations forces can be weakened and the exposure to bombing of Chinese communist lines of communications and bases can be postponed. Evidence of an all-out effort, including the expenditure of the Chinese communist Air Force, probably will be delayed as long as possible for the reasons mentioned in paragraph 2.

4. The support of public opinion in communist China for major military operations can be whipped up much more easily if it can be represented that an immediate threat to the Manchurian border exists; this notwithstanding the general assumption that Chinese communist leaders are aware United Nations forces do not intend to cross the frontier and would not attempt an invasion of Manchuria with a force of only ten divisions in any case.

5. United Nations successes to date can be most effectively countered by a crushing Chinese communist victory in North Korea, thereby enhancing Asian and communist prestige in relation to Western imperialism and eliminating as a fighting force an important part of the U.S. Army.

The above points necessarily are matters of opinion to a considerable degree, but the Chinese military on Formosa have access to more China mainland sources of information and have had more experience in this field of estimating Chinese communist intentions than others outside the Curtain; their opinions therefore warrant the most careful attention at this time.

No official in the State Department passed Ambassador Rankin's cable on to the Joint Chiefs so that they could inform the President that the Chinese Nationalists thought that "all-out action by the Chinese communists could be expected." The reason for this failure was that the contents of the cable were largely "matters of opinion" and the State Department was no longer taking the opinions of the Chiang Kai-shek regime with great seriousness.

However, at the joint Chinese–North Korean Army headquarters in Mukden, Manchuria, Marshal P'eng Teh-huai was indeed preparing to "throw the book" at the U.N. forces. Kim Il Sung, Commander-in-chief of the North Korean Army, was given public credit by the Chinese for directing operations. But P'eng Teh-huai made all the basic decisions.

P'eng was opposed by a U.N. Command of some 440,000 men. But of these, only about 100,000 were front-line troops. And as their battle dispositions were published in the world press, P'eng knew that they were stretched thin and widely dispersed.

By the third week in November, with the front still quiet, Far East Command Intelligence increased its estimates of Chinese Communist Forces in North Korea to a maximum of 70,051 and a minimum of 44,851. The calculation of these figures down to the last digit only added a further touch of unreality to them, for the actual figures might have given even General MacArthur pause.

In front of the 8th Army in the west was the XIII Army Group of the Chinese Fourth Field Army. This comprised eighteen infantry divisions of some 180,000 men. Concentrated before X Corps in the east was the IX Army Group of the Chinese Third Field Army, with twelve infantry divisions of about 120,000 men. In addition to this force of at least 300,000 Chinese, twelve divisions of the North Korean Army, numbering about 65,800 men, had recovered sufficiently to be fit to reenter combat. And about 40,000 guerrillas were operating behind the U.N. Command.

"The Chinese," as General Matthew Ridgway later wrote "was a tough and vicious fighter who often attacked without regard for casualties." The capabilities and tactics of the Chinese were perfectly suited to the terrain in which they waited. In an age of nuclear and advanced nonnuclear armaments, the Chinese infantryman could test a doctrine of Chairman Mao and his associates derived from decades of guerrilla warfare against more modern forces with superior arms: that of "man-over-weapons."

CHAPTER NINE

Reaching the Yalu

The first American soldiers to reach the Yalu did so on November 21. In the middle of that morning, three battalions of the 17th Regimental Combat Team of the 7th Infantry Division warily entered the North Korean town of Hyesanjin on the river's south bank. They encountered no opposition.

At Hyesanjin, the Americans saw nothing more ominous than a deserted military camp that had been attacked and burned by U.S. Navy carrier-based planes a week before. This and earlier aerial bombing had left about 85 percent of the town in ruins. The Americans looked across the Yalu into the snowy wastes of Manchuria and saw Chinese soldiers peacefully walking their posts. Beyond the sentries was an untouched Chinese village.

Here, the Yalu was not the great river it became near its mouth flowing into the Yellow Sea but a ribbon of ice fifty to seventy-five feet wide. The single bridge connecting Hyesanjin to Manchuria had been bombed out. To reach this narrow stretch of the Yalu, the 17th Regimental Combat Team (RCT) had moved some two hundred miles in twenty days up a winding dirt mountain road from the east coast port of Iwon. The journey had been accomplished in temperatures that often hit thirty-two degrees below zero. North Korean and Chinese resistance had been light.

A week before, the 2nd Battalion of the 17th RCT had crossed the Ungi River below Hyesanjin over an improvised oil drum footbridge. A few miles to the east the 3rd Battalion at the same time began to wade through what was thought to be ankle-deep water. But during the previous night, dams had been opened upstream by the North Koreans.

The Americans entered the water with the temperature at seven degrees below zero to find it filled with ice that came up to their waists. Before the crossing was called off and re-routed over the footbridge, eighteen men suffered frostbite. Uniforms had to be cut off them and the men wrapped in blankets and removed to the command post tent to restore their circulation.

In this kind of cold it became necessary to mix alcohol or alcohol-base antifreeze with gasoline to prevent gasoline lines from freezing. Blood plasma had to be heated for ninety minutes before it could be used. Water-soluble medicines froze, and at night sweat turned to ice inside men's boots. The 7th Division ordered the immediate delivery of five hundred oil-burning stoves and two hundred and fifty squad tents.

The 7th Division, like the other American units in North Korea, was not fully prepared for winter warfare as a result of the post-World War II wave of military economizing. Few of the soldiers had arctic parkas. Many had no gloves. They wore leather boots, but these were not insulated. Nevertheless, the 17th RCT did reach its objective.

Once standing on the banks of the Yalu, some of the American soldiers spit into the stream. General Almond, commanding X Corps, and Major General David Barr, commanding the 7th Infantry Division, appeared on the scene. They were photographed with Colonel Herbert Powell, commanding the 17th RCT, heavily bundled up and smiling, looking across the Yalu into Manchuria.

General MacArthur himself sent a message to General Almond, part of which read: "Heartiest congratulations, Ned, and tell Dave Barr that the 7th Division hit the jackpot." In congratulating Barr, Almond told him: "The fact that only twenty days ago this division landed amphibiously over the beaches at Iwon and advanced 200 miles over tortuous mountain terrain and fought successfully against a determined foe in subzero weather will be regarded in history as an outstanding military achievement."

Below the 17th RCT, other regiments of the 7th Division were advancing with dispatch on their own Yalu River objectives. Such was not the case with the 1st Marine Division, some one hundred miles to the southwest of the 7th Division. To the exasperation of X Corps headquarters, the Marines were moving up their Main Supply Route to the Chosin Reservoir at a slow, almost timid, pace not characteristic of the Corps. This, however, was deliberate.

Major General Oliver Smith, commanding the 1st Marine Division, did not share the optimism of Tokyo or the other field commanders. In fact, despite the Chinese withdrawal after their first savage battles with the Marines, General Smith smelled a rat. On November 15, he wrote a letter to the Commandant of the Marine Corps, General Clifton Cates, in which he expressed the opinion that there was no evidence that the Main Supply Route would continue to remain unmolested. General Smith's letter continued:

> Someone in high authority will have to make up his mind as to what is our goal. My mission is still to advance to the border. The Eighth Army, 80 miles to the southwest, will not attack until the 20th. Manifestly, we should not push on without regard to the Eighth Army. We would simply get further out on a limb. If the Eighth Army push does not go, then the decision will have to be made as to what to do next. I believe a winter campaign in the mountains of North Korea is too much to ask of the American soldier or marine, and I doubt the feasibility of supplying troops in this area during the winter or providing for the evacuation of sick and wounded.

Smith also wrote that although the spirit of his men was fine, he was disturbed about his "wide open left flank" and did not like the "prospect of stringing out a Marine Division along a single mountain road for 120 air miles from Hamhung [the port city and Division Command Post] to the border."

Between November 10, when the Marines reached the Koto-ri plateau, and November 23, when they neared the group of mud-thatched huts that was Yudam-ni on the southwest corner of the Chosin Reservoir, the Marine advance averaged only a mile a day. General Smith ignored the exhortations to quicken his pace from X Corps headquarters, which was reflecting the impatience of the U.N. Commander. Instead, Smith took time to prepare an airstrip for the evacuation of the sick and wounded and for the supplementation of supplies delivered by road. He also had ammunition and other critical supplies stockpiled at Hagaru at the foot of the reservoir and tried to improve the Main Supply Route so that it could be used by tanks and trucks and as a possible open and secure line of retreat.

In addition, provisions were made for the large-scale evacuation of casualties to the division hospital at Hungnam, which was enlarged to four hundred beds, and for the emergency flying of surgical teams to Hagaru. Medical clearing stations were set up along the Main Supply Route, and the *Consolation,* a hospital ship, was directed to sail to Hungnam.

General Smith attempted to concentrate the isolated forces of his division. Because of its recent battle experience at Inchon and the traditional discipline demanded by the Marine Corps, this division was the most effective fighting force the Americans had in North Korea. Only two of the 1st Division's three regiments were in forward positions. Colonel Litzenberg's 7th Regiment took up a blocking position at Yudam-ni. Fifteen miles away from them at Hagaru was the 5th Regiment under Lieutenant Colonel Raymond Murray. The 1st Regiment, commanded by Colonel Lewis "Chesty" Puller, still remained well behind, guarding the Main Supply Route back to Hamhung.

General Smith had fought with the 1st Marine Division in World War II on Guadalcanal, New Britain, Peleliu, and Okinawa. These had all been successful amphibious assaults on islands. Now the Marines were embarked on a very different type of campaign, and Smith was worried about the lack of concern at X Corps headquarters about his exposed left flank. The weather also disturbed him.

Siberia harbors the world's largest cold air mass. Bitter winds were now sweeping down from Siberia and over Manchuria to shroud the Marines in subzero temperatures. General Smith knew that many men had reported to sick bay crying, extremely nervous, and in a state of shock. The doctors had told Colonel Litzenberg that the cause was "simply the sudden shock of the terrific cold when they were not ready for it."

His exposed left flank had caused Smith concern since the advance north began. Despite his misgivings about the opportunities such exposure offered to a determined enemy, he followed orders to continue the advance. "I hoped there might be some change in the orders on the conservative side," Smith noted in his log on November 23. "This did not materialize and I had to direct Litzenberg to go on to Yudamni."

On November 27, the Marines were scheduled to move westward over a single road surrounded by dismal gorges, granite cliffs, and trackless wastes to close the wide gap between themselves and the 8th Army, which was assigned to jump off on November 24. The 7th Division was ordered to proceed northeast to the border. The movement of the 8th Army and the Marines to the Yalu was seen by General MacArthur as a "massive compression envelopment" and a "giant U.N. pincer."

In the Pentagon, as General Ridgway later observed: "There was no joy . . . at seeing our forces dispersed in the manner that MacArthur had now dispersed them." On November 21, a meeting had been held to review the situation. It was attended by Secretary of Defense Marshall, the Joint Chiefs, and Dean Acheson. Nothing came of it.

"The JCS were somewhat disturbed by the exposed position

of X Corps," General Collins later wrote, "but we took no direct action to change the situation." As a layman, Acheson expressed his private concern to Bradley and Marshall over the U.N. Commander's scattering of his forces. He was told that the Chiefs of Staff could not direct the theater commander's dispositions seven thousand miles from the front.

"But," Acheson wrote later, "under this obvious truth lay, I felt, uneasy respect for the MacArthur mystique. Strange as these maneuverings appeared, they could be another 5,000-to-1 shot by the sorcerer of Inchon. Though no one could explain them, and General MacArthur would not, no one would restrain them."

General Ridgway had somewhat the same feeling. According to him: "But in the Pentagon as well as in the field there was an almost superstitious awe of this larger-than-life military figure who had so often been right when everyone else had been wrong—who had never admitted a mistake in judgment, yet whose mistakes in judgment had been remarkably few. Then there were those who felt that it was useless to try to check a man who might react to criticism by pursuing his own way with increased stubbornness and fervor."

Overlooked, or at least left unspoken, was the simple fact that the MacArthur who had won such a deserved reputation during World War II was faced with an entirely different situation in Korea. It was not just that he was now seventy years old, or that he had very little personal knowledge of the actual ground situation in Korea. In defeating the Japanese, he had relied heavily on his air power to destroy fixed installations on islands held by relatively immobile troops. His air power also had destroyed Japanese naval forces, which could not be hidden on the seas for long. The use of naval power to launch amphibious island invasions by Marine Corps and Army troops called for a different strategy from that needed in a protracted land war.

In the mountains of North Korea, MacArthur was faced with a foe who was highly mobile, marched fast at night and hid during the day, and required few supplies. Air power

could have little effect against such an elusive enemy. In
World War II, MacArthur had the full resources of the United
States to defeat Japan, culminating in the atom bomb. Such
was not the case in Korea. Douglas MacArthur, who believed
that in war there is no substitute for victory, was probably
the last commander whom fate should have chosen to direct
a war meant to contain an aggressor rather than to defeat
him. But he was directing it and doing so under instructions
from the Joint Chiefs that allowed him considerable latitude.
Until now, he had not violated clear policy lines laid down
by Washington except for his use of non-Korean troops in the
border regions, and that had been overlooked. He was now
planning to drive right up to the Chinese border, and the
Joint Chiefs failed to impress upon President Truman the
military risks that this involved.

It was not, however, MacArthur's stature as a "larger
than life military figure" and the lack of specific warnings from
the Joint Chiefs to the President that entirely accounted for
Truman's reluctance to restrain the General. There were practical political considerations at work. In searching for an
issue that could arouse the voters against the Democrats,
Republican leaders had chosen to accuse the Administration
of being soft on communism. In particular, the foreign policy
of Dean Acheson, which gave priority to the defense of
Europe, was subjected to intense attack. In a phrase that he
would use during the 1952 campaign, Senator Richard Nixon
of California described Acheson as the "Dean of the Cowardly
College of Communist Containment."

In February, Senator Joseph McCarthy of Wisconsin had
charged Acheson with harboring "fifty-seven card-carrying
Communists" in the State Department. In April, McCarthy
declared that he would name a man "now connected" with
the State Department who was the "top Russian espionage
agent" in the United States. McCarthy's charges caused a sen-
sation and resulted in an investigation of them by a Senate
subcommittee presided over by Millard Tydings, Democrat
of Maryland. After taking two million words of testimony,

the subcommittee labeled McCarthy's charges "a fraud and a hoax." Nevertheless, McCarthy kept up his attacks. For good measure, he told the American Society of Newspaper Editors that Acheson's predecessor as Secretary of State, George Marshall, had been "pathetic and completely unfitted" for that post and his appointment "little short of a crime."

Acheson was the son of an Episcopal bishop. He attended Groton, Yale, and Harvard Law School and first went to Washington in 1919 as law clerk to Justice Brandeis. After the successful practice of law with an influential firm, Acheson served briefly as Undersecretary of the Treasury under Franklin Roosevelt. He was then Assistant Secretary of State from 1941 to 1945, Undersecretary from 1945 to 1947, and Secretary since 1949. Truman thought he was an excellent Secretary of State and a firm anti-Communist. But the attacks of McCarthy and other Republicans registered with many voters.

In the November 7 elections, the Democratic majority in the Senate was reduced from twelve to two, and cut by two-thirds in the House of Representatives. The Senator the Democrats most wanted to beat, Robert Taft of Ohio ("Mr. Republican"), won by a resounding majority of around four hundred thousand votes. Among the Democrats defeated was Millard Tydings, and the issue that chiefly beat him was the accusation that he had whitewashed the McCarthy investigation of Communist infiltration into the State Department. Senator Nixon easily won reelection by making the Democrats' failures in Asia his major issue.

In this political climate, it would be asking for trouble for Truman to step in and deny MacArthur victory, which seemed to be within his grasp despite the risks involved. The General was a Republican, and to restrain him could easily be pictured as appeasement of the Chinese Communists. The Republicans were already blaming the Democrats for the loss of mainland China to the Communists in 1949, despite the more than two billion dollars in American aid given to Chiang Kai-shek during the civil war.

Politically, the easiest way out of the Korean adventure

was to do nothing and hope for the best. This is what happened. Dean Acheson later wrote that he was "unwilling to urge on the President a military course that his military advisers would not propose." So no advice was given to the President to stop MacArthur. Truman would much later have reason to say:

> What we should have done is to stop at the neck of Korea. . . . That's what the British wanted. . . . We knew the Chinese had close to a million men on the border and all that. . . . But MacArthur was commander in the field. You pick your man, you've got to back him up. That's the only way a military organization can work. I got the best advice I could and the man on the spot said this was the thing to do. . . . So I agreed. That was my decision—no matter what hindsight shows.

As MacArthur's drive was about to begin, the United States and the United Nations continued to reassure Peking that they had, in Acheson's phrase, "no ulterior designs in Manchuria." The Chinese Communists were invited to send a delegate to the United Nations at Lake Success to discuss a MacArthur report documenting Chinese Communist intervention in North Korea in late October. Chou En-lai turned down the offer, proposing instead that the discussion should center on the "question of armed intervention in Korea by the United States Government."

In Tokyo, MacArthur, operating without any clear direction from Washington, was considering what course of action to pursue. There were only three possible courses, he concluded. He could pull his command back to the waist of the Korean Peninsula; drive on to the Yalu River; or simply remain where he was.

The latter course struck him as being absurd. It had the disadvantages of the first two and none of their advantages. A withdrawal to the waist he saw as a political disaster, since it would leave a large portion of North Korea to the control of the Communists. But to drive on to the Yalu would unify all of Korea and make possible the establishment of a democratic government, fulfilling the aims of the United Nations as set forth in its resolution of October 7. This is what the General decided must be done.

On Thanksgiving Day, November 23, the front-line troops in North Korea received a pleasant surprise. They were given a holiday meal, most of it supplied by airdrop. The meal began with shrimp cocktail and was followed by roast young tom turkey with cranberry sauce and candied sweet potatoes. Also on the menu were stuffed olives, fruit salad, fruit cake, hot coffee, and mince pie.

The next day, at 10 A.M., the 8th Army began its offensive. A confident communiqué from MacArthur was read to the troops before they moved out behind the heaviest artillery barrage of the war. The General declared that the "United Nations massive compression envelopment in North Korea against the new Red Armies operating there is now approaching its decisive effort." If it were successful, he felt that the pincer movement should "for all practical purposes end the war."

On the same day, November 24, the Central Intelligence Agency presented a National Intelligence Estimate to President Truman in Washington. According to the President, this estimate declared that the Chinese Communists would "at a minimum increase their operations in Korea, seek to immobilize our forces, subject them to prolonged attrition, and maintain the semblance of a North Korean state in being. It also stated that the Chinese possessed sufficient strength to force the U.N. elements to withdraw to defensive positions."

This C.I.A. report did not reach Tokyo until three weeks after it was received by the President in Washington, according to Major General Courtney Whitney, MacArthur's chief aide. Whitney dismissed it as being of no help in answering the "great question" of Chinese intentions in any case. In Whitney's view, the C.I.A. estimate boiled down to the statement contained in it that "available evidence is not conclusive as to whether or not the Chinese Communists are as yet committed to a full scale offensive effort."

Meanwhile, as General Whitney engaged in such thinking, and as General MacArthur issued confident communiqués and the Administration did nothing but hope for the best, some three hundred thousand Chinese Communist soldiers hidden in the snow-covered hills and valleys of the far north of Korea waited for the U.N. Command.

Three hours after its divisions moved out against very light opposition, 8th Army headquarters was visited by General MacArthur. He flew in from Tokyo especially for the occasion. At the airstrip near the Chongchon River he was greeted by General Walker, Major General Frank Milburn, commander of I Corps, and Ebbe, Milburn's dachshund.

It was a sunny morning, with the temperature at fifteen degrees. After squatting down and patting Ebbe, MacArthur pulled the hood of his pile-lined parka over his head and rode in a jeep to I Corps for a briefing. He also visited 24th Division headquarters and toured the IX Corps sector.

To Major General John Church, commander of the 24th Division, the U.N. Commander was reported by the correspondent of *Time* to have said: "I have already promised wives and mothers that the boys of the 24th Division will be back by Christmas. Don't make me a liar. Get to the Yalu and I will relieve you."

To the commander of IX Corps, Major General Coulter, MacArthur is supposed to have remarked: "Tell the boys from me that when they reach the Yalu, they are going home. I want to make good my statement that they are going to eat their Christmas dinner at home."

According to General Whitney, who was with MacArthur, what the U.N. Commander said to Coulter was of a conditional nature: "If this operation is successful, I hope we can get the boys home for Christmas." Neither Whitney nor MacArthur felt that the "home for Christmas" remarks should be taken as a prediction, although they were.

After a five-hour tour of the front, MacArthur and his party boarded the *SCAP* for the three-hour return flight to Tokyo. Despite his outward display of optimism, the General was concerned about the still unsatisfactory supply situation, the numerical weakness of the U.N. front-line troops, and the poor condition of the South Korean troops.

Thinking that a personal reconnaissance over enemy lines would be useful, MacArthur instructed his pilot, Lieutenant Colonel Anthony Story, to fly to the mouth of the Yalu, then east over the length of the river. This disconcerted Whitney, for the *SCAP* was unarmed and escorted by only a few fighter planes. As the *SCAP* approached the enemy border, Whitney noticed that its occupants cast "many a longing look" at the unused parachutes at the rear of the plane. MacArthur himself declined to put one on, reasoning that "the very audacity of the flight would be its own protection."

From an altitude of five thousand feet, MacArthur and Whitney could see below no sign of enemy activity. As the *SCAP* flew eastward along the river almost to the Siberian border, what met the eye was a quiet expanse of barren, snow-covered countryside, roads and trails that betrayed no sign of extensive recent use, and the black, partially ice-locked waters of the Yalu.

As it flew over Hyesanjin, the *SCAP* tipped its wings in a salute to the 17th Regimental Combat Team, then flew southeast to Tokyo without incident. For this audacious reconnaissance flight, the Air Force later awarded MacArthur the honorary wings of a combat pilot and the Distinguished Flying Cross.

Once back in the Dai Ichi Building, MacArthur issued another communiqué. This was a special one to the United Nations, and it exuded his characteristic confidence:

> The giant UN pincer moved according to schedule today. The air forces, in full strength, completely interdicted the rear areas and an air reconnaissance behind the enemy line, and along the entire length of the Yalu River border, showed little sign of hostile military activity. The left wing of the envelopment advanced against stubborn and failing resistance. The right wing, gallantly supported by naval air and surface action, continued to exploit its commanding position.

Our losses were extraordinarily light. The logistic situation is fully geared to sustain offensive operations. The justice of our course and the promise of early completion of our mission is reflected in the morale of troops and commanders alike.

MacArthur in turn found a message waiting for him in Tokyo. The message was from the Joint Chiefs and showed very little confidence. On the other hand, it contained no instructions to the U.N. Commander to halt his "giant pincer." The Joint Chiefs noted the "growing concern within the United Nations over the possibility of bringing on a general conflict should a major clash develop with Chinese Communist forces as a result of your forces advancing squarely against the entire boundary between Korea and Manchuria. Proposals in United Nations may suggest unwelcome restrictions on your advance to the north." However, the Joint Chiefs declared that the Administration had decided "that there should be no change in your mission, but that immediate action should be taken at top governmental level to formulate a course of action which will permit the establishment of a unified Korea and at the same time reduce risk of more general involvement."

This cautionary, yet ambiguous message also suggested that MacArthur halt his offensive on the high ground commanding the Yalu Valley. He replied at once that it would be "utterly impossible for us to stop upon terrain south of the river as suggested and there be in a position to hold under effective control its lines of approach to North Korea."

From a political point of view, he pointed out: "Moreover, any failure on our part to prosecute the military campaign through to its public and oft-repeated objective of destroying all enemy forces south of Korea's northern boundary as essential to the restoration of unity and peace to all of Korea, would be . . . regarded by the Korean people as a betrayal of . . . the solemn understanding the United Nations entered into on their behalf, and by the Chinese and all of the other peoples of Asia as weakness reflected from the appeasement of Communist aggression."

In the face of this quick and determined response, the Joint Chiefs let the matter slide. And the 8th Army offensive * continued to progress well. If it was a gamble on the part of the U.N. Commander, taken with the uneasy assent of the President, the Secretary of State, and the Joint Chiefs, the gamble appeared to be a winning one.

General MacArthur was a perceptive student of military history. In convincing his many opponents that the "5000-to-1" gamble at Inchon would succeed, he had easily cited the tactics of General James Wolfe in scaling the heights to the supposedly impregnable fortress of Quebec in 1759.

However, for all of his professed understanding of the "Oriental mind," MacArthur seemed not to have given much attention to the military theories of Chairman Mao about "luring the enemy deep." Nor did MacArthur seem to have recalled a distinction made by a general of World War II in his *Account of the War in Africa*.

"A bold operation," wrote Erwin Rommel, "is one which has no more than a chance of success but which, in case of failure, leaves one with sufficient forces in hand to cope with any situation. A gamble, on the other hand, is an operation which can lead either to victory or to the destruction of one's own forces."

The Chinese intervention and withdrawal in October had presented the world with an enigma. But there was also an enigma in General MacArthur's behavior. Why was he taking this gamble against a foe that outnumbered him five to one and whose earlier intervention he himself had said threatened his command with destruction? His severest critics could answer that his actions were those of a man determined to embroil the United States in a full-scale war with Communist China against the policy of the Administration in order to eradicate communism from China. His partisans could reply that he sincerely believed that his gamble would succeed, as

* Taken part in by the U.S. 2nd, 24th, and 25th Divisions; the ROK 1st, 6th, 7th, and 8th Divisions; the British 27th Brigade; and the Turkish Brigade; with the U.S. 1st Cavalry Division held in reserve.

it had at Inchon, and that only resolute action would forestall a second and more massive Chinese intervention.

The explanation for MacArthur's obtuseness, however, could also be that he, too, was capable of error and that he had misjudged the capabilities and intentions of the Chinese as he had those of the Japanese in December 1941. In late November 1950, while at the apex of a long and brilliant career, MacArthur may have fallen victim to his own legend. Certainly he was displaying signs of the worst sin of Greek tragedy, the sin of *hubris,* by tempting fate with an offensive that to at least one observer, Homer Bigart, war correspondent of the New York *Herald Tribune,* "made no sense. It was an invitation to disaster."

Nevertheless, MacArthur's confidence seemed to be justified as the 8th Army met little opposition for two full days after it attacked along a seventy-mile-wide front.

Early on June 25, 1950, North Korean armed forces invaded South Korea. Four days later, General of the Army Douglas MacArthur flew from Tokyo, where he directed the Allied occupation of Japan, to observe a North Korean artillery and mortar barrage on Seoul, the South Korean capital. To MacArthur's left is his intelligence chief, Major General Charles Willoughby, and next to him is Harold Noble, First Secretary of the U.S. Embassy in abandoned Seoul.

On September 15, 1950, from the bridge of the U.S.S. *Mount McKinley,* General MacArthur observes the successful amphibious landing by the U.S. 1st Marine Division at Inchon, a plan he had pushed through over the objections of the Joint Chiefs of Staff. From left: Rear Admiral James Doyle, Brigadier General E. K. Wright, MacArthur, and Major General Edward Almond, Commanding General X Corps.

Colonel Lewis "Chesty" Puller, commander of the 1st Marine Regiment and the most decorated Marine, General MacArthur, and Major General Oliver Smith, Commanding General, 1st Marine Division, observe mopping-up operations at Inchon on September 17, 1950. The landing at Inchon in the rear of the North Korean Army almost caused its destruction as an effective fighting force.

On October 1, 1950, General MacArthur sent South Korean troops across the 38th Parallel into North Korea and toward the Manchurian border. Here officers of the 3rd Republic of Korea Division, the first to make the crossing, stand with their American military advisers and display a sign marking the event. On October 7, General MacArthur sent U.S. troops across the parallel, a move that the Chinese Communists in Peking had warned would cause them to retaliate.

On October 15, 1950, President Truman, concerned about the
Chinese Communists' threats to intervene in Korea, flew to
Wake Island in the Pacific to confer with General MacArthur.

During their conference, General MacArthur told President Truman
that there was "very little" possibility of Chinese Communist
intervention. After the conference, which he termed "most
satisfactory," the President pinned an Oak Leaf Cluster to the
Distinguished Service Medal on the General's shirt.

On October 19, 1950, the Eighth Army fought its way into the North Korean capital of Pyongyang, eighty-five miles south of the Manchurian border. The next day General MacArthur flew to Pyongyang and congratulated the Eighth Army's commander, Lieutenant General Walton Walker (left). On October 24, MacArthur ordered Walker to drive to the Manchurian border, using all the troops in his command. This order violated a previous Joint Chiefs of Staff directive to MacArthur to allow the use of South Korean troops only in areas bordering China.

As the United Nations Command drove toward the Manchurian border in late October, its units began to be attacked in force by fresh troops. Those captured turned out to be Chinese. This is one of the first groups taken prisoner. They were members of the regular People's Liberation Army and had begun crossing the Yalu River from Manchuria into North Korea during the Wake Island conference.

Despite evidence of Chinese Communist intervention, General
MacArthur resumed the attack toward the Yalu River border between
Manchuria and North Korea. Here infantrymen of the 17th
Regimental Combat Team of the Army's 7th Division move through
the outskirts of Hyesanjin on the Yalu on November 21, 1950.
They were the first American troops to reach the border.

The first three Americans in the 17th Regimental Combat Team to
reach the Yalu on November 21 pause to have the historic occasion
photographed. From left, Sergeant Peter Ruplenas of South Boston,
Massachusetts, a 7th Division photographer; Corporal Mayford
Gardner of Royal Oak, Michigan; and Private First Class
Tommie Robinson of Las Cruces, New Mexico.

On November 21, 1950, the leaders of the drive that reached the Yalu stand on the frozen bank of the river separating their troops from Manchuria. From left, Brigadier General Homer Kiefer; Brigadier General Henry Hodes; Major General Edward Almond; Major General David Barr; and Colonel Herbert Powell.

On November 23, American troops in the far north of Korea were supplied by airdrop with Thanksgiving dinner. The next day the Eighth Army moved out in MacArthur's offensive to "end the war."

Two days after beginning the offensive, the Eighth Army was attacked in force by tough Chinese Communist soldiers like the captives shown here.

The U.S. Joint Chiefs of Staff were responsible for providing military advice to President Truman and direction to General MacArthur during the drive to the Yalu River and the subsequent retreat. From left, at Haneda Airport near Tokyo: General Omar Bradley; MacArthur; General Hoyt Vandenberg; Admiral Forrest Sherman; and General J. Lawton Collins.

After the death of General Walker in a jeep accident, General Matthew Ridgway (left) succeeded him as commander of the Eighth Army. Here, on March 7, 1951, MacArthur rides with Ridgway to the latter's headquarters where the U.N. Commander will hold a press conference.

On April 11, 1951, General MacArthur was dismissed from his commands by President Truman because, according to the President, "he was unable to give his wholehearted support to the policies of the U.S. Government and the United Nations in matters pertaining to his official duties." On the evening of April 17, the General arrived in San Francisco. It was the first time in fourteen years that he had been on the mainland. The next day the city was to accord him a triumphal welcome.

After delivering his "Old soldiers never die" speech to Congress on April 19, 1951, General MacArthur leaves the Capitol with his wife and their son, Arthur, to be driven to the Washington Monument grounds for still another official greeting, this time from the city of Washington. Thus ended one of America's most spectacular military careers.

CHAPTER
TEN

"An Entirely New War"

The most vulnerable element of the 8th Army in its advance toward the Yalu River was its extreme right or east flank. This was composed of the same three divisions of the South Korean II Corps that had crumpled before the brief Chinese attacks of late October.

These South Koreans moved forward smartly through rugged mountainous terrain during the first two days of the advance. But when darkness fell on November 25, they heard a sudden frightening uproar of noise. Bugles, whistles, and flutes were blown. Cymbals clanged. Drums rattled. Shepherd's pipes simulated the crowing of cocks. Mixed with all this was the shouting, laughing, and chattering of human voices.

This weird cacophony signaled the beginning of the Chinese Second Phase Offensive. When the noise stopped, the South Koreans were struck by sudden attacks. These had the intense quality described by the Chinese as *sang-meng kung-tso* or "the three fierce actions"—"fierce fires, fierce assaults, fierce pursuits."

The attacks followed a pattern known as the "one point-two sides method" developed by the Communists during the Chinese civil war. The South Koreans were allowed to enter a V formation, at whose base and both sides simultaneous assaults were directed. Meanwhile, other Chinese soldiers used draws and feeder valleys leading into the valley of the Chongchon to seal off the rear and set up roadblocks.

Earlier that morning, an infantry company of the U.S. 2nd Division had met Chinese resistance after almost reaching the top of a hill that guarded the east bank of the Chongchon River. Fighting for Hill 219 and the floodplain surrounding it continued throughout the day and into the night. But it was of an inconclusive nature, and 8th Army Intelligence did not at first appreciate that it marked the start of a major Chinese offensive. The main thrust was reserved for the South Korean II Corps.

In attempting to communicate their plight to 8th Army headquarters, the South Koreans found that their telephone lines had been cut by guerrillas and that radio communication was hindered by the mountainous terrain. By nightfall of November 27, the entire South Korean II Corps had been virtually annihilated, exposing the right flank of 8th Army.

Eighth Army headquarters made immediate attempts to protect its disintegrating right flank when it did learn something of what had befallen the South Koreans. One such attempt was an order to the Turkish Army Command Force to hold the town of Wawon in order to bolster the right flank of the 2nd Division. This was the easternmost American division of the 8th Army.

The five-thousand-man Turkish Brigade, commanded by Brigadier General Tashin Yasici, was only recently arrived in North Korea and had not yet engaged in combat. General Yasici and his staff officers had only a vague grasp of English. They often misunderstood the American orders that reached them through interpreters.

Now the newly arrived Turks found themselves alone in subzero temperatures. While trying to follow orders they did not fully understand, they were subjected to the "one point-two sides" method at Wawon. The Turks resisted bravely, withstood several Chinese attacks, and even reported the capture of two hundred Chinese prisoners. But upon their interrogation by a Japanese-American interpreter, the "Chinese" turned out to be a bedraggled and demoralized group of South Korean soldiers. They had stumbled into the Turkish lines after being routed farther north.

Without waiting for orders, General Yasici then withdrew his brigade to the southwest. This withdrawal compounded the exposure of his own east flank and that of the 2nd Division. During the withdrawal, the Chinese fell upon the Turkish Brigade with such overwhelming force that by November 27 it was destroyed as a battleworthy unit.

Elsewhere in the center and on the right of the 8th Army front the situation became desperate. General Walker reported to General MacArthur that the 8th Army was under attack by at least two hundred thousand Chinese. These Chinese were not engaging in the brief probing attacks of late October, but in a major offensive designed to envelop and destroy the entire 8th Army. Faced by an enemy of overwhelming numbers, and supported by an inadequate supply system and a reserve force lacking depth, Walker had only one choice. He must retreat.

On November 28, General MacArthur, who four days before had confidently proclaimed the beginning of an offensive to end the war, now radioed the Joint Chiefs of Staff: "The Chinese military forces are committed in North Korea in great and ever-increasing strength. . . . We face an entirely new war. . . . My strategic plan for the immediate future is to pass from the offensive to the defensive with such local adjustments as may be required by a constantly fluid situation."

Confronted with "an entirely new war," MacArthur ordered Generals Almond and Walker to report to him in person by flying from their command posts in North Korea to Tokyo. From 9:50 P.M. of November 28 to 1:30 A.M. the next day, MacArthur, Willoughby, Whitney, Hickey, Walker, and Almond conferred at the U.N. Commander's residence at the American Embassy.

At Wake Island, General MacArthur had told President
Truman that there was "very little" possibility of the Chinese
entering the Korean War. MacArthur's Intelligence Chief,
General Willoughby, had informed the United Nations Security Council on November 1 that "there is no positive evidence
that Chinese Communist units, as such, have entered Korea."
Now this long emergency meeting in Tokyo ended with the
conclusion that both the 8th Army and X Corps would have
to retreat in the face of massive Chinese Communist attacks.
MacArthur, however, preferred describing the retreat as "a
movement in retrograde."

Almost at the same time that this conference took place,
there was an emergency meeting of the National Security
Council in Washington. President Truman called it after first
learning of the debacle suffered by the 8th Army in a telephone
call from Marshall at 6:15 A.M. on November 28.

General Bradley, speaking for the Joint Chiefs, began by
summarizing the still fluid military situation and saying that it
would have to be clarified before new directives were sent
to MacArthur. But the General would obviously have to turn
to the defensive and make do with the troops under his command as new ones were not available. Bradley also recommended against bombing Manchurian airfields, as this would
invite retaliation against American planes crowded on Korean
airfields.

Marshall said' that the three armed services still agreed
that it was essential to keep the conflict limited to Korea
and not do anything that would entangle the United States,
with or without the United Nations, in a general war with
China.

Vice-President Alben Barkley, who seldom had much to say
at National Security Council meetings, wondered if Mac-
Arthur's comment about "getting the boys home for Christmas" was meant as "an incredible hoax" for the Chinese.
The President told Barkley that he would have to make his
own interpretation of the statement. But Truman did tell his
Vice-President that damage to MacArthur's prestige could

not be afforded, and nothing should be done to "pull the rug out from under the General."

Dean Acheson, who felt that the United States was now closer than ever to a wider war, said that some way should be found to end the conflict. Meanwhile, the State Department would attempt to unite the pro-Western delegations in the United Nations against the Chinese Communists and have their activities labeled as aggression despite the certainty of a Soviet veto in the Security Council.

All the military men present were disturbed by the exposed and scattered tactical position of MacArthur's divided command. However, this meeting ended as so many earlier ones had. The Joint Chiefs made no specific recommendations to the President for correcting the situation. MacArthur was left to get out of the predicament he was in as best he could.

The General would never admit that he was in this predicament because he had allowed his forces to blunder into a trap. According to MacArthur, he had surprised the Chinese and sprung a trap they had laid. This upset the enemy's timetable, which called for massing his armies in secret for a spring offensive that would destroy the U.N. Command in one blow. By acting as he had, MacArthur felt that he had saved his command from eventual annihilation.

This version of what had happened was echoed by General Whitney, who later wrote: ". . . he was not taken by surprise. His troops did *not* rush blindly north into a massive ambush as claimed by some detractors. The big push north had been carefully designed to be effective either as a mopping-up operation or as a reconnaissance in force and now it had unhappily become the latter."

This evaluation was probably first voiced by General Walker. On November 29, Walker told the press: "The assault launched by the Eighth Army five days ago probably saved our forces from a trap which might well have destroyed them. . . . The timing of our attack to develop the situation was, indeed, most fortunate."

As Walker spoke, his 8th Army was beginning the longest

retreat in the history of American arms. Sudden Chinese night onslaughts split the United Nations forces into small, beleaguered units fighting their way out of what bore every resemblance to an ambush or trap.

The infantry regiments of the U.S. 2nd Division had the worst time of it. As the 8th Army began its offensive, the U.S. 24th Division was positioned in the far west, the 25th Division in the center, and the 2nd Division in the east, a few miles above the town of Kunu-ri. The Chinese Second Phase Offensive did not bother with the 24th Division. But it struck the rest of the front along the corridor of the Chongchon Valley. Particular violence was directed at the South Korean II Corps on the east flank of the 2nd Division. The Chinese intended to sweep behind the exposed 2nd Division, press west to the Yellow Sea, and thus trap the entire 8th Army.

General Walker ordered the 24th and 25th Divisions to fall back fifty miles to Pyongyang, the North Korean capital, which had been captured on October 19. The 2nd Division was given the assignment of covering this retreat by holding the Chinese turning movement to the west at Kunu-ri.

Under constant and punishing Chinese attacks, some of the besieged, confused, and leaderless troops of the 2nd Division surrendered or broke in panic and fled, first giving rise to the phrase "bugout fever." But most of the men held their rear-guard positions as the 24th and 25th Divisions attempted to withdraw south under less severe pressure.

The commander of the 2nd Division, Major General Laurence Keiser, whose own command post had come under fire, was ordered to withdraw his forces after five days of ceaseless fighting in subzero temperatures. On December 1, the division started to move south from Kunu-ri to the town of Sunchon. From there another road led to Pyongyang.

There was a narrow defile and a pass between two cliffs along the road to Sunchon. As the lead American vehicles approached the mouth of the pass, they were blown apart by Chinese mortars. The pass became a corridor into hell as the Americans continued the attempt to move through it. An entire Chinese division was entrenched on ridges for five miles north of the pass, pouring down a murderous storm of steel on the men and vehicles below. As night fell on December 1, General Keiser's men were still cut off at the pass. It was not until dawn the next morning that four thousand of Keiser's troops cleared the bottom of the pass with the aid of American air strikes and a British ground force. Three thousand Americans—dead, severely wounded, or captured—were left behind.

The captured men had good reason to fear the worst. During the first five months of the war, the North Koreans had frequently tied the hands of captives behind their backs and shot them in the head. Others had died of malnutrition or disease in makeshift prison camps. The behavior of the Japanese had often been savage toward Western captives in the Second World War. Now another Oriental enemy was taking American prisoners on a large scale.

Instead of being shot or kicked in the teeth, however, the Americans were greeted by the Chinese with a smile, a handshake, and the offer of a cigarette. Often an English-speaking officer would tell the captives that they could now become "fighters for peace." This unexpected treatment produced feelings of relief but also reactions of confusion or bewilderment. The Americans had no way of knowing that the "lenient" attitude was the beginning of the various processes known in official Chinese Communist terminology as *szu-hsiang kai-tsao*—"ideological reform" or "thought reform." For the first time in United States history, her soldiers were encountering an enemy who was not satisfied to win only a battlefield victory. The Chinese Communists intended to extend the battle into the prison camps that they established along the Yalu River. The Chinese object was not to torture or brutalize their American prisoners. Rather it was to convince them through techniques of constant repetition, harassment, and humiliation that the policies of the United States Government were wrong.

The 8th Army in the west, from which the first large group of prisoners was taken, was attacked before X Corps in the east. When X Corps learned what had happened in the west, its first order was to the 17th Regimental Combat Team to withdraw from its exposed position in the far northeast at Hyesanjin. The first American unit to reach the Yalu had been congratulated by General MacArthur for having "hit the jackpot." Now, after a brief rest, the soldiers of the 17th RCT suddenly found themselves fighting their way back from the Manchurian border.

Another American unit reached the Yalu River. This was Task Force Kingston, commanded by a twenty-one-year-old second lieutenant from Brookline, Massachusetts, Robert Kingston, who was an infantry platoon leader in the 7th Division. On the evening of November 21, Kingston was ordered to spearhead an advance from Wondokchang to Singalpajin on the Yalu, a distance of thirty-two miles. Once at Singalpajin, Kingston was to establish contact with the 17th RCT, fifteen miles to the west at Hyesanjin.

Kingston began his assignment on the morning of November 22 with the thirty-three infantrymen of his platoon. They were supported by seven tracked vehicles mounted with machine guns and rapid-fire guns, which made the basic platoon a task force. Riding on the vehicles' carriages that mounted the guns and wearing woolen long johns, and scarves under their helmets to protect their ears from the cold, the infantrymen were driven forward slowly over icy roads surrounded by a snow-covered barren landscape.

When the sun shone, the temperature might rise to twenty degrees below zero. Thirty to forty degrees below zero were more normal temperatures, and weapons had to be fired periodically to keep them in working condition. The task force met no Chinese troops as it moved forward, but was harassed by remnant North Korean troops. As it fought off the North Koreans, the task force kept picking up more American troops and odd pieces of equipment. By the time it was ten miles from the Yalu, it had added two tanks, howitzers, mortars, and jeep-mounted machine guns and grown to a force of about three hundred men, including three captains, several first lieutenants, and a major. But even though Kingston was a second lieutenant, he remained in command of his assignment.

On the morning of November 28, the task force reached a small destroyed bridge eight miles from Singalpajin. From here, Kingston could see the cliffs of Manchuria and the gorge of the Yalu River. He led his soldiers across the bridge after the engineers repaired it, but they were soon stopped again by part of a cliff the North Koreans had blown apart into the road.

Since it would take the engineers a long time to clear this roadblock away, the impatient Kingston led a force of about twenty infantrymen down a cliff and across country. Soon they neared some houses on the outskirts of Singalpajin. From one of them came a volley of rifle fire, kicking up the snow and forcing Kingston to crawl into a ditch for cover. He then decided to lead a charge against the house.

Whooping and yelling, carrying his rifle in his left hand and a grenade in the other, Kingston ran over the hard-crusted snow. The cold brought tears that stung his eyes, and his breath came in aching gasps. Nearing the house, he tossed his grenade toward it and was watching the grenade arch through the air when a bullet creased the top of his helmet, spun him around, and knocked him down and out.

When Kingston came to, he saw a sergeant named Van-retti bending over him.

"You're all right, Lieutenant," Vanretti said. "You're going to be fine. We got them. That grenade came in perfect."

"Anybody hurt?" Kingston asked.

"Not a one, nobody."

"How many were there? In the house."

"Five," Vanretti said. "We got them. We thought they got you."

A company of Americans who had marched through the cleared roadblock appeared, and the task force cleared the rest of Singalpajin. Light resistance was offered by the North Koreans, who then fled across the Yalu into Manchuria.

In the afternoon, the men of the task force had a chance to

look at the river. Kingston saw a frozen sheet of ice, solid enough to support tanks. While encamped during the night, he and his men could hear the rumble of motor convoys from the other side of the Yalu. Apart from that, everything appeared to be going according to schedule.

The next morning, November 29, Kingston received a radio message from battalion headquarters. It was not a message of congratulations, but an order to withdraw south immediately. Of all the American units that attempted to reach the Yalu, Task Force Kingston and the 17th RCT thus had the distinction of being the only two that had made it. Now they were both retreating in haste from the border, not realizing that the 8th Army one hundred and fifty miles to their southwest had come under heavy attack by the Chinese and that the 1st Marine Division and the Army's 7th Division to their southeast were undergoing a harrowing experience around the Chosin Reservoir.

At the Pentagon's communications center in Washington, teletype circuits from Tokyo were chattering steadily with reports of these major reverses. On Thanksgiving Day, victory in North Korea had seemed almost complete. Less than a week later, President Truman was being informed by the Joint Chiefs that the United Nations forces were driven back and might be encircled and destroyed by the Communist Chinese.

The President's demeanor was tense as he faced more than two hundred newsmen at his regular weekly news conference on the morning of November 30. Truman opened the news conference by reading from a prepared statement. "Recent developments in Korea," he said, "confront the world with a serious crisis. The Chinese Communist leaders have sent their troops from Manchuria to launch a strong and well-organized attack against the United Nations forces in North Korea." But Truman went on to declare that U.N. forces were determined to fight to the bitter end for justice and world peace.

After reading his prepared sttaement, the President spoke informally in answer to questions. Asked if the U.N. Command would be allowed to bomb targets in Manchuria, he replied that he could not answer that question this morning. He then remarked that "we will take whatever steps are necessary to meet the military situation, just as we always have."

One of the reporters asked if that would include the atomic bomb.

"That includes every weapon that we have," the President replied.

"Mr. President," the reporter persisted, "you said 'every weapon that we have.' Does that mean that there is active consideration of the use of the atomic bomb?"

"There has always been active consideration of its use," replied Truman, who had authorized the use of two atomic bombs against Japan at the close of World War II. "I don't want to see it used. It is a terrible weapon, and it should not be used on innocent men, women and children who have nothing whatever to do with this military aggression. That happens when it is used."

The President closed his press conference with words of praise for both Acheson and MacArthur. The General was now coming under some newspaper criticism for the sudden reversals, but Mr. Truman said that he was "continuing to do a good job." These kind words were forgotten in the furor that arose over Truman's informal remarks about the use of the atomic bomb.

Some of the correspondents who heard the remarks interpreted them to mean that General MacArthur or other military leaders would be allowed to decide whether or not the bomb should be employed. Delegates to the United Nations were startled. The French Government issued an authorized statement that references to the bomb had alarmed members of the National Assembly in Paris.

In Great Britain, which had provided the largest military contribution to the United Nations apart from the United States and the South Koreans themselves, one hundred Labor Members of Parliament sent a letter to Prime Minister Clement Attlee to protest the possibility of the bomb's use. The leader of the Opposition, Winston Churchill, was alarmed and let it be known that he wanted assurance that what was now happening in Korea would not touch off a major war. In Churchill's view ". . . the United Nations should avoid by every means in their power becoming entangled inextricably in a war with China. . . . the sooner the Far Eastern diversion . . . can be brought into something like a static condition and stabilised, the better it will be. . . . For it is in Europe that the world cause will be decided. . . . it is there that the mortal danger lies."

Prime Minister Attlee decided to fly to Washington for a conference with President Truman to clear up the confusion. Underlying the fears caused by the President's remarks was the common knowledge that while the Communist Chinese did not have the atomic bomb, their Russian allies did. Truman was obliged to issue a clarifying statement through Press Secretary Ross that emphasized that the use of the atomic bomb was still subject to the President's approval and that he had given no such approval.

This statement calmed the furor sparked by Truman's informal words at the press conference, but no sooner had this happened when the President began to encounter difficulties with the words of General MacArthur.

Defeat was unfamiliar to the General, and it did not sit well with him. He declined to accept the responsibility for it and moreover seemed bent on placing the blame elsewhere. On November 30, MacArthur sent a message to *The New York Times* columnist Arthur Krock justifying his drive to the Yalu. On December 1, the General replied to a query from Hugh Baillie, president of the United Press, with the opinion that he was "fighting against military odds without precedent in history."

On the same day, the magazine *U.S. News and World Report* released the text of an earlier interview with MacArthur. In it, the editors asked him: "Are the limitations which prevent unlimited pursuit of Chinese large forces and unlimited military attack on their bases regarded by you as a handicap to military operations?"

The General replied: "An enormous handicap without precedent in military history." Other messages in a similar vein soon followed to the Tokyo press corps, the *London Daily Mail,* and the International News Service.

This stream of public pronouncements infuriated President Truman, who saw in them an attempt by MacArthur to suggest to world opinion that "if only his advice had been followed all would have been well in Korea." The President again thought of relieving the General, but instead of doing so he issued a presidential order that all American diplomats and military commanders abroad stop "direct communication on military or foreign policy with newspapers, magazines or other publicity media in the United States."

Truman's general order, issued on December 5, was meant specifically for General MacArthur, who, according to the President, "had to be told that the kinds of public statements which he had been making were out of order." Wake Island's spirit of "complete unanimity" was now shattered.

Before this order was issued, emergency meetings on dealing with the new developments had been hastily called in Washington. At 11 A.M. on December 1, President Truman briefed congressional leaders in the Cabinet Room. He told them that the Administration's major concern was to prevent "this affair in Korea from becoming a major Asiatic war," and that the United States was not now in a position "to assume the burdens of a major war."

A joint State-Defense meeting was held in the Pentagon on the same date. Dean Acheson, who attended, felt that: "A state of panic seemed to exist at the United Nations; complaints were being made that U.S. leadership had failed."

No direct action resulted from this Pentagon meeting. The Joint Chiefs were unable or unwilling to send any new and forceful directive to the commander directing the battle. They did agree not to accede to MacArthur's repeated request to bomb Chinese supply lines and bases in Manchuria, for they again felt that this would enlarge a war that was still meant to be a limited one.

However, Secretary of Defense Marshall told the Army

Chief of Staff, J. Lawton Collins, to fly to Tokyo to confer
with MacArthur and then fly on to Korea to consult with the
field commanders there. Collins later wrote that this was done
because it was "difficult for authorities in Washington to get
a clear picture of the rapidly changing conditions in Korea."
In Acheson's blunter opinion, the reason was that MacArthur's
reports were "so confused and confusing."

In Tokyo, General MacArthur had also been holding conferences with his principal aides. These included Almond and
Walker, who were summoned from the front. At a command
conference on December 1, it was initially felt that the North
Korean capital of Pyongyang could be held by the United
Nations. However, MacArthur soon realized that his forces
could be saved only by further disengagement and the conse-
quent lengthening of the Chinese supply lines, which would
diminish the force of their offensive.

The General had developed the conviction that it was not
his strategy but treachery that lay behind the Chinese successes.
He felt that some leak in intelligence was evident. Walker, according to MacArthur, continually complained to him that
his operations were known to the enemy in advance through
sources in Washington.

"I will always believe," the United Nations Commander
later wrote, "that if the United States had issued a warning to
the effect that any entry of the Chinese Communists in force
into Korea would be considered an act of international war
against the United States, that the Korean War would have
terminated with our advance north. I feel that the Reds would
have stayed on their side of the Yalu. Instead, information
must have been relayed to them, assuring that the Yalu bridges
would continue to enjoy sanctuary and that their bases would
be left intact. They knew they could swarm down across the
Yalu River without having to worry about bombers hitting
their Manchurian supply lines."

MacArthur never offered any concrete evidence to support
his suspicions, nor did his aide General Whitney. However,
Whitney presumed that the traitors were the officials in the

British Embassy in Washington, Burgess and MacLean, who were soon to defect to the Soviet Union. As his aide observed MacArthur wondering at his lack of support and the "curious antics in Washington," Whitney felt that it was "almost as if the highest officials were conspiring against him."

In the Pentagon, another urgent meeting was held on December 3. The possibility that all American forces would have to be evacuated from Korea was seriously considered. This meeting took place "amid deepening gloom," according to Acheson, who was informed by the Joint Chiefs that in two or three days a crisis would be reached. Acheson then went to the President and urged him to declare a state of national emergency. Such a proclamation would underscore the gravity of the situation for the American people, and enable Truman to institute wage and price controls, higher production goals, and a sizable increase in the armed forces. The President took Acheson's plea under serious consideration.

The deepening gloom at the Pentagon had been caused by a message received from MacArthur on December 3. The message contained a chilling conclusion. The United Nations Commander reported that X Corps was being withdrawn to the port of Hungnam and that the 8th Army must withdraw to Seoul, twenty-five miles southeast of the 38th Parallel. Both withdrawals would continue "unless ground reinforcements of the greatest magnitude are promptly supplied."

MacArthur described the combat effectiveness of the South Korean troops as being negligible, and all of the troops under his command as being understrength and "mentally fatigued and physically battered," except for the U.S. 1st Marine Division. He felt that the Chinese attackers were "fresh, completely organized, splendidly trained and equipped and apparently in peak condition for actual operations."

The General further reported that the "directives under which I am operating based upon the North Korean Forces as an enemy are completely outmoded by events." He saw himself facing "the entire Chinese nation in an undeclared war" and concluded that "unless some positive and immediate action is taken, hope for success cannot be justified and steady attrition leading to final destruction can reasonably be contemplated."

The Joint Chiefs had no ground reinforcements of "the greatest magnitude" with which to supply MacArthur, and they had already declined his request to bomb Manchuria. Faced now with his prediction of "final destruction," they took his message to the President. Truman then authorized the Joint Chiefs to send this immediate reply to Tokyo:

> We consider that the preservation of your forces is now the primary consideration. Consolidation of forces into beachheads is now concurred in.

MacArthur did not believe that this was all that could or should be done. He began to formulate plans for "positive and immediate action" for repulsing the Chinese attacks and winning the war, which he would shortly submit to Washington. Meanwhile, it was up to men on a much lower level of strategy to determine whether the battered 8th Army in the west and especially the forward elements of X Corps around the Chosin Reservoir in the east could be preserved.

CHAPTER
ELEVEN

The Strategic Retreat

Lieutenant Colonel Don Faith's journey toward the Yalu River began on November 25. He was then in the port of Hungnam, where he heard a radio broadcast from MacArthur's Tokyo headquarters announcing the start of a United Nations offensive to end the war.

Faith listened to the cheering prediction that American troops would be returned to Japan by Christmas. He and the 1053 men of his 1st Battalion, 32nd Infantry Regiment* then huddled into trucks and were driven eighty miles over the twisting Main Supply Route to the southeastern tip of the Chosin Reservoir. Along the way, a dry snowfall mixed with road dust to send yellowish clouds billowing around the trucks.

Despite this annoyance and the stinging cold, the morale of the Army infantrymen was high. They all thought that the war would soon be over. The Tokyo radio broadcast had reinforced this belief. However, when they reached the light-blue sheet of ice that was the "Frozen Chosin" on November 26, the new-

* This unit was part of the Army's 7th Division, which was part of X Corps along with the 1st Marine Division.

comers were given some less cheerful information by Marine units they relieved.

On their own way to the reservoir, the Marines had been attacked from November 2 to November 7 by Chinese troops, who then withdrew. On November 26, the Marines captured three Chinese enlisted men who agreed that the 58th, 59th, and 60th Divisions of the 20th Field Army were in the area with orders to cut the Main Supply Route. Colonel Faith therefore took the precaution of arranging his battalion in defense perimeters, but nothing happened that night.

The next day, November 27, was also uneventful. Since it was still quiet at 9 P.M., Faith asked his company commanders to report to him to receive their attack orders for dawn. The orders from X Corps, commanded by General Almond, were for the 1st Battalion to secure a road that curved along the eastern shore of the reservoir and then join the Marines who had grouped on its western shore, in a pincer movement toward the Yalu River fifty miles to the north.

As the officers were discussing these orders in the command post, which was established in a farmhouse in a valley near the reservoir, the battalion's outer defense positions were attacked. When the Americans lit up the dark night by firing at the Chinese, they faded away. This was only because the Chinese were at first attempting to draw fire in order to pinpoint the Americans' positions.

Shortly after midnight, the Chinese launched a full-scale attack. Corporal Robert Lee Armentrout, operating a heavy machine gun, saw a group of Chinese charging at him up a steep ridge. Armentrout could not lower the gun enough to hit his attackers. He picked it from its tripod and beat off the Chinese by swinging the barrel at them like a large metal baseball bat. Elsewhere, the Chinese killed Captain Edward Scully, commander of Company A, with a grenade. Faith sent Captain Robert Haynes to replace Scully. Chinese infiltrators killed Haynes before he reached his men.

When other infantrymen were not fighting off Chinese, they

sat numbly in their holes with sleeping bags pulled up to their waists. There were no warm-up tents within the defense perimeter. The cold was so severe that light machine guns had to be worked by hand to fire single rounds because their automatic-firing mechanisms froze.

When light broke, the Chinese withdrew. Faith saw that despite heavy manpower losses, his battalion had held most of its position. He realized that there was now no question of advancing toward the Yalu River. Instead of attacking during the morning of November 28, the colonel tried to regain the ground lost during the night fighting.

A helicopter landed in a rice paddy near the command post in the afternoon. General Almond himself stepped from the copter. The X Corps commander, who often toured the front lines, discussed with Colonel Faith the situation facing the 1st Battalion. Almond then told Faith that he had three Silver Stars in his pocket. One of the medals, which was awarded for gallantry in action, was for the colonel. He was asked to select two soldiers to be awarded the others.

Faith saw Lieutenant Everett Smalley sitting on a water can behind him. Smalley was a platoon leader who had been wounded the previous night. He was now awaiting evacuation.

"Smalley," the colonel called out, "come over here and stand at attention."

As Smalley did so, Sergeant George Stanley, a mess sergeant, wandered by.

"Stanley," Faith ordered, "come here and stand at attention next to Lieutenant Smalley."

Faith then had some dozen men—clerks, truck drivers, and walking wounded—line up behind Stanley and Smalley to witness the presentation. General Almond pinned the medal, a bronze star with an oak wreath and small silver star at its center, to the parkas of Faith, Stanley, and Smalley, shook their hands, and then spoke to the entire group.

Those present remembered the X Corps commander saying, in effect: "The enemy who is delaying you for the moment is nothing more than the remnants of Chinese divisions fleeing north. We're still attacking and we're going all the way to the Yalu. Don't let a bunch of Chinese laundrymen stop you."

Almond walked over to a jeep, spread out a map on its hood, and, while gesturing northward, engaged in a brief discussion with Faith. The General then reentered his helicopter. As the craft rose from the ground, Faith ripped the Silver Star from his parka and threw it into the snow. He walked back to the command post with his operations officer, Major Wesley Curtis.

"What did the General say?" Curtis asked.

"You heard him," Faith muttered. "Remnants fleeing north."

Lieutenant Smalley returned to his water can and sat on it. "I got me a Silver Star," he said to one of the soldiers present at the ceremony, "but I don't know what the hell for."

When night fell, Faith did not prepare his battalion to attack "all the way to the Yalu." Instead, he got it ready to beat off another Chinese attack, even though he had no way of knowing that one would take place. By now, the battalion aid station, located in a two-room farmhouse, was so crowded that more than a dozen wounded men huddled outside of it awaiting medical treatment. This treatment was necessarily primitive. The nearest M.A.S.H.—the mobile army surgical hospital created to perform emergency, lifesaving surgery and render its patients transportable to rear hospitals—was operating one hundred miles to the south. No one had foreseen that a M.A.S.H. would be needed around the Chosin Reservoir.

About twenty frozen corpses were laid out in front of the battalion aid station. Eventually, the bodies, accompanied by an emergency medical tag, would be evacuated south to a central collecting point, where they were embalmed and fingerprints taken. Permanent interment in Korea was not the policy of the U.S. Quartermaster Corps. Packed in ice, bodies were shipped to Japan, where they were totally embalmed, put in military caskets, and shipped on to the United States for burial near the soldier's home or in a military cemetery.

Other bodies were interred in division cemeteries in Korea. These were lowered into an open grave, face up, encased in a mattress cover that held a burial bottle containing a report of interment. The grave was closed and a temporary marker placed over it. But these bodies, too, were eventually dug up and shipped back to the United States.

The personal effects of those killed were inventoried by their commanding officer and sent to the rear through channels until they reached the Effects Center at Kansas City, Missouri. There they were checked again and transmitted to the next of kin. If the money carried by the deceased was worth $4.99 or less—regardless of whether it was in dollars, military scrip, *won,* or *yen*—it was sent along with his effects. If the money was worth $5.00 or more, it was converted into a United States Government check.

Colonel Faith had no time to inventory the personal effects of the corpses lying in front of the battalion aid station, for about four hours after darkness fell the Chinese launched another massive assault. Lieutenant James Campbell, a platoon leader in Company D, shot a Chinese running at him when the soldier was ten feet from his foxhole. As Campbell shouted orders to a machine-gun crew, he was knocked down. He felt no pain, but thought that he had been hit in the face with a hammer. Instead, a bullet-sized mortar fragment had gone through his cheek and stuck in the roof of his mouth. Campbell kept on fighting along with his machine-gun crews.

While the night fighting was going on, General Almond was conferring with General MacArthur in Tokyo. The United Nations Commander decided that X Corps must withdraw to the south. The order reached the 1st Battalion at about 3 A.M. of November 29. About an hour before dawn, Colonel Faith's men began to march south down a road skirting the reservoir; about a hundred wounded were hauled on trucks. Their objective was Hagaru, some fifteen miles south. Here the Marines had established a solid defense perimeter that included a hospital, supply dumps, and an airstrip for light aircraft.

After proceeding for about four miles, Faith's men ran into a Chinese roadblock. They fought through it to find themselves on low ground, on one side of which was the reservoir and on the other three high ridge-lines, all occupied by Chinese. The Americans were surrounded, with their rations almost gone and their gasoline supplies and ammunition running low. Squeezed into a new defense perimeter of about six hundred by two thousand yards, they fought off the Chinese, sustained by the hope that a force would break through from the south and rescue them.

Only two developments saved these Americans from being destroyed on the afternoon of November 29. One was the tactical air support provided by the black Corsairs of the Marine Corps. The carrier-based Corsairs scourged the enemy constantly with machine-gun fire, rockets, and napalm bombs. The Corsair pilots later reported that they could drop their loads effectively anywhere around the defense perimeter because there were so many Chinese in the area. The other saving factor was the airdrop of rations and ammunitions.

However, no relief column had appeared by daybreak of December 1. At 10 A.M., a Marine fighter-bomber flew over the surrounded defense perimeter. The pilot radioed down that he would guide more planes in for an air strike shortly after noon. He also said that he could see no relief column on the eleven miles of road between Faith's forces and Hagaru.

Instead of taking the risk of being overrun by another night of Chinese attacks, Faith decided to try to reach Hagaru in a breakout timed for 1 P.M. to coincide with the air strike. As the lead elements moved out, four Marine planes appeared to give them close support. But the planes missed the Chinese with their napalm bombs, whose orange flames enveloped and incinerated many Americans instead.

Faith's units, which had retained their organizational structure until now, broke apart into leaderless groups. Most of the officers and noncommissioned officers had been killed or wounded. The survivors had not slept for four days, since it was realized that anyone who fell asleep would freeze to death. But they kept moving south.

Just before dark, the Americans encountered another road-block. Colonel Faith led about one hundred men against the roadblock and knocked it out. But in this action, Faith was hit by grenade fragments. He was carried to a truck and placed in its cab. There, sometime during the night, he died, and by the next afternoon his body was frozen. His command disin-tegrated into wretched little bands of frostbitten and wounded men united by desire to survive rather than by discipline. The first stragglers began arriving in Hagaru during the night of December 1.

One of the them was Lieutenant Campbell, who arrived at the Marine hospital at 5:30 A.M., December 2. In addition to having a swollen cheek and mouth caused by the mortar frag-ment lodged in the roof of his mouth, Campbell's left leg and side had been sprayed by mortar fragments early in the morn-ing of December 1. During the breakout, Campbell had also jumped out of a truck and then watched three other trucks roll over an embankment. He had listened helplessly to the screams of the wounded inside the trucks, who were spilled or crushed.

Despite all this, Lieutenant Campbell did come out alive. By December 4, when most of its survivors had reached Ha-garu, the 1st Battalion, 32nd Infantry numbered 181 officers, men, and attached South Korean troops out of the original 1053 who had started out for the Yalu River on November 25. Don Faith was later awarded the Congressional Medal of Honor.

On December 4, Prime Minister Attlee arrived in Washing-ton and at four in the afternoon began his talks with Presi-dent Truman. On the same date, General Collins arrived in Tokyo. He had brief discussions there with MacArthur and then flew on to General Walker's 8th Army headquarters in Seoul, landing at dusk. That evening, the Army Chief of Staff began his attempt to clarify at first hand the fluid military situation for the Administration and the Joint Chiefs in Washington.

When Collins arrived in Seoul, the only thing that was certain was that the drive to the Yalu River had failed and that there was no hope of successfully resuming it in the foreseeable future. In the west, the battered 8th Army was in retreat and could be trapped if the Chinese could sustain their attacks. Forward Army elements and the 1st Marine Division were surrounded by twelve Chinese divisions at Hagaru and were still some sixty miles from the eastern seacoast.

Despite this grim overall picture, Collins concluded, after being filled in by Walker on developments following the Chinese offensive, that the disaster predicted by MacArthur was not inevitable. Some of his retreating units were badly hurt, Walker reported, but others remained in relatively battleworthy condition. If Walker were ordered to hold Seoul and the area north of the Han River, he felt that the 8th Army might be threatened with encirclement. On the other hand, a withdrawal all the way back to the old Pusan perimeter, from which the 8th Army had started its drive north in mid-September, would give it a line it could hold indefinitely.

The next day, December 5, Collins reconnoitered the battle zones with Walker and the following day prepared to fly to X Corps headquarters at Hamhung to obtain General Almond's assessment of his situation. Before he boarded his plane at Kimpo Airfield in Seoul, newsmen asked Collins if the United States would employ the atomic bomb as a tactical weapon against the Chinese.

"Certainly not from what I saw yesterday," the Army Chief of Staff replied.

He was also asked if it were possible for the 8th Army to be encircled by the Chinese driving down its right flank.

"I think," Collins said, "the Eighth Army can take care of itself."

Upon arriving at Hamhung, Collins was advised by Almond that X Corps could be concentrated in beachheads within the next few days and evacuated from them by the Navy without great difficulty, if necessary. Collins agreed with Almond. Their estimate was made while the 1st Marine Division was still surrounded by Chinese some sixty miles north of the seacoast. And the object of the Chinese, as documents captured from them later indicated, was to "annihilate" the Marines.

As Faith's army battalion on the southeastern shore of the Chosin Reservoir was attacked by the Chinese on the night of November 27, the two Marine regiments under Colonels Litzenberg and Murray on the southwestern shore at Yudam-ni were also attacked. In the pitch-black night, the silent hills around the Marines suddenly came alive with thousands of Chinese in green or mustard-yellow padded-cotton uniforms.

The Chinese pattern of attack was designed to offset the enemy's advantage in arms and equipment by employing surprise, superior numbers, and a mobility derived from being unburdened with transport and heavy weapons. Small combat groups of Chinese foot soldiers peeled off from their larger tactical columns, one at a time, and closed in on the entrenched Marines with grenades, rifles, and submachine guns. Appearing to rise out of the very earth, the Chinese either struck the American positions frontally or crept and wriggled around them in infiltration attempts.

Once fired upon, the attackers hit the ground, came on again at the first lull, and kept up their assault with no regard for casualties, who were quickly replaced. The Chinese met death stoically, often stumbling forward over carpets of their own corpses as they sang Oriental chants. Because they moved on foot without tank or air support, without transport except for a few shaggy Mongolian ponies, and with hardly any weapons bigger than a mortar, the Chinese were able to take the most primitive and unsuspected routes of approach.

The Marines at Yudam-ni were fourteen miles north of Hagaru. The lifeline of the Main Supply Route between these two points was cut by the Chinese on the morning of November 28, isolating the seven thousand men of the 5th and 7th Regiments. But the Marines fought off three Chinese divisions

of thirty thousand soldiers, reopened the road, and gained
Hagaru. The last elements of the rear guard entered the supply base at 2 P.M. on December 4. About fifteen hundred
casualties were brought to Hagaru. Almost one-third of them
had been disabled by frostbite. The evacuation of the wounded
by air to Hungnam began as the 1st Marine Division regrouped
for its march back down the Main Supply Route to the sea.

News reports from Korea created doubts as to whether the
Marines could fight their way out as an organized force, or
at all, and presented an equally disturbing picture of the 8th
Army's situation in the west. Typical was the comment of
Newsweek, which told its readers that what was now taking
place in North Korea represented "America's worst licking
since Pearl Harbor. Perhaps it might become the worst military
disaster in American history."

Time informed its readers that: "It was defeat—the worst
defeat the United States ever suffered. The Nation received
the fearful news from Korea with a strange-seeming calmness
—the kind of confused, fearful, half-believing matter-of-fact-
ness with which many a man has reacted upon learning that
he has cancer or tuberculosis. The news of Pearl Harbor, nine
years ago to the month, had pealed out like a fire bell. But the
numbing facts of the defeat in Korea seeped into the national
consciousness slowly out of a jumble of headlines, bulletins,
and communiqués; days passed before its enormity finally became plain."

General MacArthur read these news reports and others in
a similar vein and took exception to them. "Such quotations,"
he later wrote to the 1st Marine Division's deputy chief of staff,
"certainly do not reflect the mood of the American public at
the time, but rather the emotional reaction of irresponsible
writers. . . ." To MacArthur, what was now happening was
"one of the most successful strategic retreats in history, com-
parable with and markedly similar to Wellington's great Peninsula withdrawal."

MacArthur's own treatment by the American and European
press must have nettled a man of his strong ego. It also might

have spurred him to develop aggressive plans for retaliation against the Chinese in order to recoup his reputation. In searching for a scapegoat, much of the press singled out the General. For the first time in his distinguished career, he suddenly found himself being criticized as a military incompetent. An editorial of December 6 in the New York *Herald Tribune,* an influential newspaper of Republican persuasion, blamed MacArthur for "one of the greatest military reverses in the history of American arms," because he had "compounded blunder by confusion of facts and intelligence."

The editor of the *Reader's Digest,* DeWitt Wallace, and his staff abruptly stopped the presses at their printing plants in Dayton, Ohio, and Concord, New Hampshire, after they had printed a third of the eleven-million-copy run of the January issue. The lead article in this issue was to have been about MacArthur's victory in Korea and was entitled "The Right Man in the Right Place."

In North Korea itself, Major General Oliver Smith became annoyed by news reports that the Marine Corps was retreating for the first time in its history. Smith had never liked the MacArthur strategy, which directed the 1st Marine Division to advance through subzero temperatures to the Manchurian border widely separated from the 8th Army. The Marine general had taken precautions to deal with just such an emergency as had now arisen. To a group of correspondents who had been flown into Hagaru on December 4, Smith said: "Retreat, hell! We're not retreating, we're just advancing in another direction." The commander of the 1st Marine Regiment, Colonel Lewis "Chesty" Puller, remarked: "We'll suffer heavy losses. The enemy greatly outnumbers us. They've blown the bridges and blocked the roads . . . but we'll make it somehow." Puller, winner of four Navy Crosses and the most decorated member of the Marine Corps, was a blunt man with a belligerent thrust to his jaw who strode about with his chest thrown out like a bantam rooster.

At 7 A.M. on December 6, "Chesty" Puller and the other Marines, along with attached units of the American and South

Korean armies and 235 commandos of the British Royal Marines, began a running fight to the sea. They were trailed by thousands of homeless Korean refugees emitting low-pitched wails of misery. Along the way, the United Nations force was supplied by airdrops from the Air Force's Combat Cargo Command. These included the parachuting of eight spans of a 16-ton bridge to replace a crucial bridge blown by the Chinese.

The bearded, sleepless men, existing on canned rations which were kept from freezing by body heat, crunched south over crisp snow, accompanied by their crawling vehicles. The twisting, single-lane road they used was flanked on both sides by Chinese, who poured murderous fire down upon them. To aid the wounded, Navy medical corpsmen had to melt morphine syrettes in their mouths before giving injections. Because blood plasma could not be kept from freezing even when warmed against the body, the corpsmen had to watch men die for the lack of it. The wounded were all evacuated by air. This left no available space to evacuate the dead. At Koto-ri, six miles south of Hagaru, one hundred seventeen Marines, soldiers, and Royal Marine Commandos were pushed into a mass grave by bulldozers on December 8. That night, Navy corpsmen assisted two Korean refugee women to give birth.

However, by 9 P.M. of December 11, all of the units that had started out on the march to the sea had reached the safety of the defense perimeter in the Hamhung-Hungnam port area. Battle and nonbattle casualties claimed about one-third of the force, but the Chinese had failed to achieve their objective. As a document captured from the Chinese 20th Army put it: "We succeeded in the separation and encirclement of the enemy, but we failed to annihilate the enemy one by one. The units failed to carry out the orders of the higher echelon. For example, the failure to annihilate the enemy at Yut-an-ni [Yudam-ni] made it impossible to annihilate the enemy at Hakalwu-ri [Hagaru]."

The reason for the Chinese failure would become obvious after the shock caused by their initial success wore off. They were simply not a modern fighting force and lacked the means to exploit the advantage given to them by surprise and superior numbers. "Marine tanks, artillery, mortars, rockets and machine guns reaped a deadly harvest, and still the enemy kept on coming with a dogged fatalism which commanded the respect of the Marines," the Corps' official history later commented, describing the casualties endured by the Chinese as "frightful."

These casualties could be replaced, but supplies of food and ammunition could not be replaced quickly by human and animal transport. After failing to achieve their objective in four days, the steam went out of the Chinese attack. In battle, their communications system of bugles, whistles, and flares proved to be no substitute for radios. The primitive Chinese medical system could not handle the crippling effects of frostbite, the night blindness caused by vitamin deficiency, gangrene caused by neglected frozen limbs, and the high incidence of tetanus resulting from the improper care of wounds.

A document captured from the Chinese 27th Army complained that: "The troops did not have enough food, they did not have enough houses to live in, they could not stand the bitter cold, which was the reason for the excessive non-combat reduction in personnel (more than 10,000 persons), the weapons were not used effectively. When the fighters bivouacked in snow-covered ground during combat, their feet, socks, and hands were frozen together in one ice ball; they could not unscrew the caps on the hand grenades; the fuses would not ignite; the hands were not supple; the mortar tubes shrank on account of the cold; 70 per cent of the shells failed to detonate; skin from the hands was stuck on the shells and the mortar tubes."

The Chinese 26th Army concluded that a shortage of transportation and escort personnel made it impossible to supply its troops. "As a result, our troops frequently starve," one of its captured documents read. "The troops were hungry. They ate cold food, and some only had a few potatoes in two days. They were unable to maintain the physical strength for combat; the wounded personnel could not be evacuated. . . . The fire power of our entire army was basically inadequate. When we used our guns there were no shells and sometimes the shells were duds."

Slowed by supply weaknesses and riddled by casualties, the Chinese were unable to prevent the evacuation from Hungnam. The Army's 7th and 3rd Divisions manned a defense perimeter around the small port, in whose harbor waited a vast armada of ships ranging from freighters to aircraft carriers assembled from every available source in the Far East. The Chinese had no air force or navy capable of attacking these ships. As embarkation began, the port area rocked to violent explosions as tents, trains, bridges, and unsalvageable supplies and vehicles were destroyed, sending great masses of orange flames swirling brilliantly up into the sky.

On December 11, General MacArthur was flown to Yongpo Airstrip just south of Hungnam. This was his first visit to Korea since October 21. He approved the evacuation plan of X Corps, which, if it were successful, would eventually land X Corps at the old Pusan perimeter and see it transferred to control of the 8th Army.

MacArthur was then flown on to Seoul to confer with General Walker. Since the start of the Chinese Second Phase Offensive, the center of the 8th Army line had been driven back about seventy-five miles. Some of its units had taken a fearful mauling; the U.S. 2nd Division alone suffered five thousand casualties, one-third of its authorized strength. Morale was low. In the surprise and chaos of retreat, sizable American and South Korean units broke under fire and ran away.

As bad as the near-disaster was, it became evident to MacArthur and Walker that the 8th Army, like X Corps, had escaped entrapment. Walker's motorized columns had managed to outrace the pursuing Chinese foot soldiers. A new defense line was established along the 38th Parallel just north of Seoul. But the Chinese in mid-December failed to attack this line, which caused some puzzlement to the American commanders.

There was really no puzzle about this halt. As had been true at Chosin Reservoir, the Chinese lacked the modern transport needed to follow up and finish off their initial success. But they were now bringing men and supplies down from Manchuria in supply trains that included ox carts, North Korean porters, and Bactrian (two-humped) camels. During this ominous pause, the Administration was given time to consider what course of action to take next while the Chinese assembled for a Third Phase Offensive.

CHAPTER TWELVE

A State of National Emergency

From the beginning of the Chinese onslaught through the lull of mid-December President Truman did not lack for counsel on what to do in Korea. He was, of course, continually supplied with counsel by the State Department and the Pentagon. But as soon as the situation changed and bordered on disaster, influential Republicans began to offer a steady barrage of advice to the President.

On December 2 in Washington, Senator Joseph McCarthy demanded that Truman accept Generalissimo Chiang Kai-shek's offer to send Chinese Nationalist troops into battle against the Chinese Communists in North Korea, a course also advocated by General MacArthur. This demand confronted Truman with a serious dilemma, for he did not want to "unleash" Chiang. There was no reason to believe that Chiang's troops could improve upon their sorry performance against the Communists in the Chinese civil war; they could be more usefully employed in the defense of Formosa; and their entry into North Korea would cost the United States considerable support in the United Nations. McCarthy, and his demand, however, could not be dismissed lightly.

The thirty-seven-year-old Wisconsin Republican was just beginning to become a major factor in national affairs. He had first attracted wide attention on February 9 with a speech at Wheeling, West Virginia. McCarthy then claimed, although he never produced any evidence to support the claim, that he held in his hand "a list of two-hundred and five that were known to the Secretary of State as being members of the Communist Party and who nevertheless are still working and shaping the policy of the State Department."

On December 2, McCarthy, who regarded MacArthur as "the greatest American that was ever born," declared: "If this treasonable farce of insisting that only American boys can die, while refusing the help of the soldiers of our Allies continues, then the time is long overdue for the Congress, in the name of America, to stand up and be counted and immediately impeach you, Mr. President."

Senator Henry Cabot Lodge, Republican of Massachusetts also urged Truman on December 2 to send Chinese Nationalist troops to North Korea. Lodge did not, however, demand the President's impeachment if this were not done. As both Senators delivered their opinions, Wellington Koo, the Chinese Nationalist Ambassador to the United States, said that Chiang's troops were ready to march "if the United Nations would approve." The United Nations did not and never would approve.

On this December 2, President Truman decided to observe his scheduled attendance at the annual Army-Navy football game. He traveled by rail from Washington to Memorial Stadium in Philadelphia under extreme security measures that had not been used since World War II. As the presidential train arrived in Philadelphia, Secret Service agents pounced on two men in the waiting crowd. One of them had been heard to say in a loud voice: "If I had a gun I could bump him off from here." The detainees, Michael Panszylowski and Adolph

Ruzcyk of Lackawanna, New York, were released after the Secret Service decided that they were only engaging in a form of macabre humor. Truman stayed until the end of the football game, which was won by an underdog Navy team, 14 to 2.

Upon his return to Washington, the President prepared for his conference with the British Prime Minister. A few hours after Attlee's arrival in Washington on December 4, Senator William Knowland, Republican of California, stood on the floor of the Senate and asked that the Prime Minister state whether the United States must face the Chinese Communists "alone."

Knowland was unhappy with what he considered the disinclination of the United Nations, and the British in particular, to take a hard line against the Chinese Communists. This hesitancy Knowland blamed on "the concentrate-on-Europe clique."

"America has been faced with dark days before," the Senator said. "We hoped to meet any future ones with stanch allies in the common cause of freedom, not just regional freedom, Mr. Prime Minister. But if we have to meet them alone perhaps it is better to find it out now. If others want to clasp the hand of the murderer and welcome him into their home we don't have to stultify ourselves to that extent."

Knowland called for renewed military aid to Chiang Kai-shek, the instant expulsion of Soviet Russia from the United Nations, and demanded that the United Nations "untie" the hands of General MacArthur so that he could bomb Chinese supply and marshaling areas in Manchuria.

On December 5, Senator Taft, the unchallenged leader of the Republican Party on Capitol Hill and its most likely presidential candidate in 1952, called on President Truman to give the American people "more complete information" about what was going on in North Korea. Taft declared that there was a good deal of public confusion about the present crisis that might be clarified if the President would "state what the problems are." On the same day, a Democratic Senator, James Eastland of Mississippi, demanded the resignation of Dean

Acheson. Four ladies of the Anti-Communist League delivered a petition with signatures, said to be a block long, to Senator McCarthy's office calling for the Secretary of State's removal from office.

On December 7, a Gallup poll revealed that 55 percent of the American people believed that World War III had started. The next day, Governor Thomas Dewey of New York, the defeated Republican presidential candidate in 1944 and 1948, said that this was not the time "for further criticism" of the Administration's Far Eastern policies in view of the "state of national emergency" that had arisen. Dewey also said that the New York State Civil Defense Commission had mailed a letter to all "non-target areas" requesting these areas to assume their share "of a possible million evacuees" in case an atom bomb was dropped on New York City.

As Governor Dewey spoke, Prime Minister Attlee concluded his talks with President Truman. Privately, Attlee had been assured by Truman that he would not authorize the use of atomic bombs in Korea or downgrade the American commitment to defend Western Europe. In a public communiqué issued at the White House, the two leaders said that there could be no thought of appeasement in Korea, but they were willing to negotiate with Communist China for a peaceful solution to the fighting on "the basis of a free and independent Korea."

Meanwhile, at Lake Success, the United Nations debated the issue of the Chinese Communist intervention in North Korea and what to do about it. The Chinese Communists were heard on the subject of their intervention, even though they had not been admitted to a United Nations seat. Nine delegates from the People's Republic of China had been invited to attend meetings of the U.N. Security Council, primarily to discuss the Formosa question.

Heading the delegation was General Wu Hsiu-chuan, director of the Eastern European and U.S.S.R. Division of the Peking Foreign Office. When Warren Austin, the U.S. delegate, asked him to explain why his country had intervened in North Korea, General Wu was neither contrite nor conciliatory.

There was no reason why he should be, since the Chinese held the upper hand from the immediate military viewpoint.

In the course of a long and vitriolic speech, Wu accused the United States of instigating the Korean War to further "its fanatical design of dominating Asia and the world."

"Who has shattered security in the Pacific?" General Wu asked the Security Council. "Have Chinese armed forces invaded Hawaii, or have United States armed forces invaded . . . Korea and Formosa? . . . The real intention of the United States, as MacArthur has confessed, is . . . to dominate every Asiatic port from Vladivostok to Singapore."

Wu demanded that the United Nations force the United States to withdraw from Korea and Formosa, but said that whether this was done or not, the People's Republic of China would chase off "U.S. aggressors."

Confronted with this kind of language, the President could see no hope that the Chinese would solve the Korean problem by withdrawing or even agreeing to a cease-fire. And there was very little that could be done to force them out of Korea without embarking on an all-out war, as Acheson had advised Truman during the Attlee talks.

The pressure of this dilemma upon Truman was perhaps what caused him to lose his temper when his daughter's ability as a singer was evaluated unfavorably by Paul Hume, music critic of the Washington *Post,* after Miss Truman gave a concert in Washington. The President wrote a letter to Hume on White House letterhead, which contained phrases such as: "I have just read your lousy review buried in the back pages. You sound like a frustrated old man who never made a success, an eight-ulcer man on a four-ulcer job, and all four ulcers working.

"I never met you, but if I do you'll need a new nose and plenty of beefsteak and perhaps a supporter below. Westbrook Pegler, a guttersnipe, is a gentleman compared to you. You can take that as more of an insult than as a reflection on your ancestry."

General MacArthur read the account of this incident that

appeared in *The New York Times* of December 9 and was "shocked" by it. The General, as he later wrote, "had noted with growing concern his [the President's] increasingly indecisive handling of the Korean situation." The strong language in Truman's letter to Hume meant to MacArthur that: "It was quite apparent his nerves were at a breaking point—not only his nerves, but what was far more menacing in the Chief Executive of country at war—his nerve."

The grim news from Korea was not the only pressure on Truman in early December. For though it appeared possible that the Americans could be driven out of Korea, it appeared certain at the same time that the French in Indochina could not avoid a humiliating defeat by Ho Chi Minh's Vietminh insurgents in North Vietnam. French authorities ordered the evacuation of all French women and children from the Red River Delta and Hanoi in the face of a major Vietminh offensive.

Ho Chi Minh was recognized by Russia and China as the legitimate ruler of an independent republic, while France and the United States recognized the Emperor Bao Dai. To the Vietminh, who considered themselves nationalists, Bao Dai was a puppet manipulated by the French to shore up colonialism. The Vietminh troops were being trained in South China, and military supplies were sent to them across the common border between China and Indochina.

Their common allegiance to communism was not the only bond that tied Vietnam inextricably in with China. North Vietnam had been part of the Chinese empire for a thousand years down to the tenth century. After breaking free of Chinese rule, North Vietnam remained in the Chinese cultural orbit, using the Chinese writing system, studying the Confucian classics, modeling Vietnamese political and family life, literature and thought, on China.

The United States, anxious not to disturb its relationship with France in Europe, backed what was beginning to look like a losing cause in Vietnam. However, plagued by manpower requirements in Korea, President Truman refrained from sending American troops to Vietnam. American involvement was limited to military supplies given directly to the French through a Military Assistance Advisory Group (MAAG) and economic assistance given directly to the Bao Dai Government.

Meanwhile, advice from all quarters on how he should deal with the immediate problem in North Korea continued to be offered to the President. On December 12, Joseph P. Kennedy, former U.S. Ambassador to Great Britain, gave a speech before the University of Virginia Law Forum in Charlottesville. Kennedy claimed that American foreign policy was "politically and morally a bankrupt policy" that had "solidified communism" and failed to establish a strong defense in the Western Hemisphere. The former ambassador said that the United States should get out of Korea, and strengthen its defenses "in Canada, in the Caribbean, and in Latin America."

President Truman had not responded to his critics or made any new public policy statements by December 14. On that date, Governor Dewey gave a major foreign policy address at the Waldorf-Astoria Hotel in New York City. Dewey declared that the nation's prestige was "very low" and called upon it to undertake the greatest mobilization in its history to combat Communist aggression. The Governor demanded that the National Guard be federalized "tomorrow morning," that universal military service for every young man be instituted without delay, and that an eighty-group Air Force and a one hundred-division Army be created.

"If we are not prepared to fight for our freedom," the Governor said, "then we shall surely lose it. If we are prepared to fight, we still could win." At Lake Success, fifty-two U.N. delegates, including Warren Austin, voted in favor of a resolution proposed by thirteen Middle Eastern and Asian states authorizing a three-man committee to try to arrange a cease-fire in Korea. This was a public retreat from the General Assembly's resolution of October 7, which had sanctioned the use of military force to achieve the political objective of establishing an independent and unified Korea.

On the same day, Moscow radio broadcast the North Korean communiqué: "On all fronts, units of the People's Army waged battles against American and South Korean troops." Peking issued no communiqué for the Communist Chinese position remained that no regular units of the People's Liberation Army were fighting in North Korea, only Chinese volunteers.

On December 15, at the darkest moment of the Korean War —which neither the United States nor China had acknowledged was a war—President Truman finally prepared to tell the American people that their country was faced with a crisis. At 10:30 P.M. he was scheduled to broadcast a speech from the White House over all major television and radio networks and the global radio network of the Voice of America. But before he spoke, the President was harassed by the Republican opposition with another problem.

Secretary of State Dean Acheson was scheduled to depart in two days for Brussels, there to attend a conference of the Foreign Ministers of the North Atlantic Treaty Organization. Acheson was to discuss with America's Western European allies the common measures to be taken for the defense of that area. The Secretary of State would have to overcome the objections of some nations, principally France, to the admission of West German soldiers into the NATO plan. Almost on the eve of his departure for Brussels, Republican members of Congress voted no confidence in Acheson by overwhelming majorities. They demanded that Truman remove the highest officer in his cabinet in the name of national unity.

The President was angered by this demand, which he attributed to men "who kept repeating the completely baseless charge that somehow Acheson had brought about the Communist victory in China; they now charged that it was Acheson who was depriving General MacArthur of the means of gaining victory." Truman refused to dismiss Acheson, whose prestige in Brussels and Peking was hardly enhanced by this public attempt to get rid of him.

When he went on the air that night, the President was talking to an electorate that was for the most part confused, angered, and frustrated by a sudden, unexpected turn of events wherein the "home by Christmas" offensive had collapsed into a major reverse at the hands of a backward, largely agricultural country with no recent history of military success. Truman said that the United States would "continue to uphold, and if necessary, to defend with arms the principles of the United Nations." But he could offer no specifics about what the United States would do to repulse or punish the Communist Chinese. For although he could not say so publicly, he knew that as he spoke the United States did not have enough military power to eject the Communist Chinese from Korea while making an effective contribution to the defense of Western Europe against Soviet Russia.

The President blamed Russia, rather than China, for the "great danger" now confronting the United States as he asked the American people to turn to the ways of austerity. He announced wage and price controls and a plan to increase the armed forces from 2½ to 3½ million men within the next few months. He named Charles E. Wilson, president of General Electric, as director of a newly created Office of Defense Mobilization. Wilson was given powers to rearm the United States exceeding those held by any previous war mobilizer. In line with these measures, Truman would announce in the morning the existence of a state of national emergency.

On the morning of December 16, the President received a telephone call from Undersecretary of Defense Robert Lovett at the Pentagon. Unidentified planes, Lovett said, had been sighted on radar screens north of the American continent. Were they Russian planes, en route to drop atom bombs on American cities? The possibility that the Third World War was about to start had to be considered by the President. Alert signals were flashed to Air Force bases. Fighter planes in New England flew north to reconnoiter.

After calling Truman, Lovett telephoned Acheson in the State Department. "When I finish talking with you," Lovett told the Secretary of State, "you cannot reach me again. All incoming calls will be stopped. A national emergency is about to be proclaimed. We are informed that there is flying over Alaska at the present moment a formation of Russian planes headed southeast. The President wishes the British ambassador to be informed of this and be told that he and Mr. Attlee should take whatever measures they think are proper for Mr. Attlee's safety."

Acheson was skeptical about the accuracy of the report of a formation flight of Russian planes. As it developed, Lovett was later able to inform the Secretary of State and the President that there had been error. Some unusual atmospheric disturbance had caused those reading the radar screens to mistake a flight of geese for Russian bombers.

After this false alarm, the President took a step on December 18 to underscore the determination of the United States to rebuild Western Europe's defenses. He announced the appointment of the president of Columbia University, Dwight Eisenhower, as Supreme Commander, Allied Powers, Europe.

The Supreme Commander, Allied Powers, in Japan and Commanding General, U.S. Army, Far East still held to his opinion that the struggle between international communism and democracy would be resolved in Asia, and not in Europe. And following MacArthur's rigid logic, it was in Asia that the United States was now engaged in a war with the largest Communist nation on earth, China.

On December 22, six Soviet-built MIG jets, flown by pilots whose nationality was unknown to U.S. Air Force intelligence, were shot down by Sabre jets over the mouth of the Yalu River in the biggest air battle thus far of the war. About twenty of the remaining MIGs then flew back to their base in Manchuria. The Sabre jets were forbidden to pursue them.

This restriction was a constant frustration to General MacArthur. He would never admit that his command was being granted a form of sanctuary, too. The Russians, should they throw the full power of their potent Air Force into the battle on behalf of their Chinese ally, could inflict terrible losses upon American air installations in Japan and South Korea. To counter such a massive attack, the United States had, in the description of Hoyt Vandenberg, the Air Force chief of staff, a "shoe-string" air force.

On the same day that this aerial battle took place over the Yalu, the Premier and Foreign Minister of the People's Republic of China denounced the three-man United Nations committee seeking a cease-fire in Korea as an illegal group. Chou En-lai, in a broadcast over Radio Peking, said that his government would not negotiate with the cease-fire committee and named Communist China's demands for peace in Korea: (1) The removal of the United States Seventh Fleet from Formosan waters; (2) the withdrawal of foreign troops from Korea; (3) a seat for Communist China in the United Nations.

These terms were unacceptable to the United Nations, so the Chinese continued their military action in North Korea. However, as had been the case since early December, this activity was largely concentrated on building up the Chinese forces for the launching of their Third Phase Offensive. General Walker's 8th Army in turn waited and braced for the assault.

On December 23, Walker left his headquarters in Seoul to present a citation to the 27th British Commonwealth Brigade at Uijongbu. He rode in a specially built jeep with a handrail, a rack for his shotgun, and a red plaque bearing the three gold stars of his lieutenant general's rank. As Walker's jeep tried to pass two halted trucks on a narrow road north of Seoul, a South Korean truck suddenly pulled out without warning from behind the stationary vehicles. There was a head-on crash, and then Walker's jeep careened into a telephone pole and overturned.

The 8th Army commander was pulled from the wreck and rushed to a nearby U.S. Army field hospital, where he died shortly afterward. Walker's senior commander in World War II, George Patton, had also been killed in an auto accident, near Mannheim, Germany, five years before in the same month.

To replace Walker, President Truman designated Lieutenant General Matthew Ridgway, who had been closely following the unfolding events in Korea as Deputy Chief of Staff for Operations and Administration at the Pentagon. Truman took the advice of the Joint Chiefs and Marshall, who knew that MacArthur had already told Collins that he wanted Ridgway to succeed Walker should anything happen to the latter officer.

Ridgway, a member of the class of 1917 at West Point, served in Tientsin, China, as a young officer and in World War II commanded the 82nd Airborne Division in Normandy and Sicily. He emplaned for Tokyo after brief conferences in Washington, arriving at Haneda Airport shortly before midnight, December 25. Before going to bed, he reviewed the notes he would need for his conference in the morning with General MacArthur, who was in Ridgway's opinion "one of the few geniuses it has been my privilege to know."

In Washington on Christmas morning, President Truman learned that the last naval convoy had debarked from the smoking rubble of Hungnam the evening before, completing the successful evacuation of the 105,000 men of X Corps. "I wish to express my thanks," Truman wrote MacArthur, "to you, Admiral Joy, General Stratemeyer, General Almond and all your brave men for the effective operation—it is the best Christmas present I've ever had."

At 9:30 A.M. on December 26, Ridgway met with MacArthur in the latter's office in the Dai Ichi Building. General Doyle Hickey, MacArthur's chief of staff, was the only other person present. Ridgway had known, and admired, the United Nations Commander since he was superintendent of West Point in 1920 and Ridgway was an instructor there.

As he conferred with him now, Ridgway was again deeply impressed by the force of MacArthur's personality and the lucid and penetrating quality of his explanations and analyses. The newly arrived 8th Army commander felt that he was "a great actor too, with an actor's instinct for the dramatic—in tone and gesture."

Ridgway's genuine admiration was not unqualified, however. He thought that MacArthur had acted like "Custer at
the Big Horn" in driving toward the Yalu and that, as Ridgway later wrote, "MacArthur's all-too-human weaknesses,
which marked him as a man rather than a demigod, seemed
occasionally to have been granted him in overgenerous pro-
portion, too." Ridgway thought that the United Nations Commander was "completely misguided" in his reading of Chinese
intentions and that "his refusal to accept the mounting evidence of massive Chinese intervention was largely responsible
for the reckless scattering of our forces all over the map of
Korea."

As he discussed the present situation with Ridgway now,
MacArthur complained that the command was operating in
what he described as a "mission vacuum," while the diplomats
groped toward a solution.

"A military success will strengthen our diplomacy," Mac-
Arthur said, but the most he hoped for was "inflicting a
broadening defeat making possible the retention and security
of South Korea."

Ridgway entertained the notion of launching an offensive
when he arrived in Korea, and the last question he asked the
United Nations Commander was: "If I find the situation to my
liking, would you have any objections to my attacking?"

"The Eighth Army is yours, Matt," MacArthur replied.
"Do what you think is best."

Ridgway then conferred with members of MacArthur's
general headquarters staff and flew on to Korea, arriving at
Taegu at four o'clock of a chilly afternoon. He paid immediate courtesy calls on President Rhee and U.S. Ambassador Muccio. Wearing a hand grenade strapped to his
paratrooper's harness, Ridgway then began a tour of the
battlefronts to talk with field commanders and determine the
condition of the 8th Army.

What he discovered caused Ridgway to abandon any
thought of attacking at this time. "Every command post I

visited," he later wrote, "gave me the same sense of lost confidence and lack of spirit." The enlisted men he solicited gripes from "all conveyed to me a conviction that this was a bewildered army not sure of itself or its leaders, not sure what they were doing there, wondering when they would hear the whistle of that homeward bound transport."

Ridgway set about attempting to restore this demoralized 8th Army to a fighting mood and make it ready for the Chinese offensive that he was almost certain would begin on New Year's Day. To counter the offensive, Ridgway would have to make do with the forces he had inherited from Walker. From the start of what he had termed "an entirely new war" on November 28 until December 28, MacArthur had received no new directive from Washington on how he should deal with it or any indication that he could expect reinforcements. Moreover, Congress had still issued no declaration of war. But whatever was taking place in Korea, a police action or a new kind of limited conflict, it resembled an old war in that people on both sides were being killed and maimed.

One of those maimed was Private First Class Bob Smith, who became a frostbite casualty in the fighting around the Chosin Reservoir on November 27. He was flown to Washington from Japan on December 27. The next day, his mother, Mrs. Clara Smith of Middleburg, Pennsylvania, was flown to Washington in a chartered plane provided by the American Legion. She then visited her twenty-year-old son at Walter Reed Hospital. PFC Smith would survive, although both of his hands were gone and both of his legs were amputated below the knees. He was the first American quadruple amputee of the Korean conflict.

In Washington, the question of a new policy directive to be sent to MacArthur in Tokyo had been discussed since the day after Christmas by President Truman, Marshall, Bradley, Acheson, and Assistant Secretary of State Dean Rusk. A final draft was agreed upon and sent to the United Nations Commander on the morning of December 29. The main points of the long directive were later briefly summarized by Acheson:

1. If with present UN strength, we could resist at some point in Korea without our incurring serious losses, and if the apparent military and political prestige of Chinese Communists could be deflated, it would be of great importance to our national interests.

2. "In the face of increased threat of general war" the Joint Chiefs would not commit additional U.S. ground forces in Korea. Major war should not be fought in Korea.

3. "Therefore . . . your directive now is to defend in successive positions, subject to safety of your troops as your primary consideration, inflicting as much damage to hostile forces in Korea as is possible."

4. Decision was to be made ahead of time by the Joint Chiefs on the last reasonable opportunity for orderly evacuation. General MacArthur's views were requested on the conditions which should determine evacuation.

MacArthur interpreted this directive as an indication on the Administration's part of a loss of the "will to win" in Korea. To him it meant that Washington was not considering methods of counterattack, but "the best way to run." The United Nations Commander felt that if he were allowed to "use my full military might, without artificial restrictions, I could not only save Korea, but also inflict such a destructive blow upon Red China's capacity to wage aggressive war that it would remove her as a further threat to peace in Asia for generations to come."

Late in the evening of December 30, MacArthur composed a long reply to the new policy directive, which he sent to Washington. The reply included four proposals for retaliatory measures against Communist China: "(1) blockade of the coast of China; (2) destroy through naval gunfire and air bombardment China's industrial capacity to wage war; (3) secure reinforcements from the Nationalist garrison on Formosa to strengthen our position in Korea if we decided to continue the fight for that peninsula; and (4) release existing restrictions upon the Formosa garrison for diversionary action, possibly leading to counter-invasion against vulnerable areas of the Chinese mainland."

MacArthur had received no answer to his proposals as night fell upon Korea on New Year's Eve. The United Nations Command was established along a 135-mile-long front just north of the 38th Parallel and numbered some 365,000 men, including troops from fourteen other nations besides the United States and South Korea. According to General Willoughby, MacArthur's intelligence chief—who was still keeping to his practice of supplying figures down to the last digit—they were faced by a total Communist force of 443,406 men. This included 276,173 Chinese and 167,233 North Koreans, with 650,000 Chinese reinforcements believed to be in Manchuria and another 250,000 en route there.

During the waning hours of New Year's Eve, the waiting troops of the United Nations Command heard the stillness along the parallel broken by the clanging of cymbals and the blowing of flutes, whistles, and bugles.

CHAPTER
THIRTEEN

Third Phase Offensive

Reports received by General Ridgway throughout New Year's Eve left him in no doubt that the Chinese Third Phase Offensive had begun. It struck with such force that he thought the 8th Army might not be able to contain it. The east flank held by South Korean units quickly collapsed.

At dawn of New Year's Day, 1951, Ridgway headed toward this sector in a jeep. A few miles north of Seoul he ran into the South Koreans in full retreat. They were packed into trucks and had abandoned all of their artillery, mortars, and machine guns and thrown away most of their rifles. The General thought in dismay that their only idea was to get as far away as possible from the Chinese who were at their heels.

He jumped from his jeep and stood in the middle of the road, waving his arms in an attempt to halt the fleeing columns. Ridgway soon abandoned this effort, realizing that "the only solution was to let them run" and stop their flight by having roadblocks set up farther down the line.

The Chinese were trying to destroy all of the U.N. forces, and Ridgway judged that they would succeed if he kept his command in its present forward positions. So he ordered a retreat across the Han River to new defense positions seventy miles south of the 38th Parallel, hoping that the Chinese attack would eventually run out of momentum. On January 3, the evacuation of Seoul was begun, and President Rhee and his cabinet abandoned their capital for the second time.

Two fifty-ton floating bridges over the Han River linked Seoul to the south. To speed the movement of military traffic, use of these bridges had to be denied to civilian refugees. On the morning of January 4, Ridgway stood at the north end of the main bridge observing the military traffic flowing south. He also observed what he later described as "one of the great human tragedies of our time." In a wind so cold that it seared his face like a blowtorch, the General watched hundreds of thousands of Korean refugees running and stumbling south over the ice that choked the Han River. He saw women carrying babies in their arms, men carrying their aged grandparents on their backs, other men bent under the weight of A-frames containing their entire family possessions.

Ridgway remained at the bridge until dark, when the last of the heavy U.N. armor crossed safely to the south bank. The last vehicle to cross was a British Centurion tank so heavy that it caused the pontoon bridge to sag deep into the ice-filled water. The general then got into his own jeep and was driven south. Behind him, the two bridges were blown up, and the Chinese entered the South Korean capital, from which masses of flame rose into the night sky.

The Chinese pressed their pursuit aggressively, without regard for casualties, and with considerable skill and flexibility at the platoon and company level. The situation looked grave for the U.N. Command on January 9, but by then the Chinese did run out of momentum. The Third Phase Offensive had, in fact, failed to trap the 8th Army or drive it into the sea, although neither Ridgway, MacArthur, nor the Joint Chiefs could be certain of this at the time.

This Chinese offensive, like the previous two, petered out because it depended on human and animal transport for supplies. When supplies ran low, the Chinese had to halt and wait for replenishment before attacking again. And the lack of modern communications equipment caused a certain tactical rigidity above the company level.

While the Chinese paused, the 8th Army, no longer susceptible to surprise attacks, took up strong defensive positions and brought its superior firepower into play. Unopposed fighter-bombers of the U.S. Fifth Air Force scourged the Chinese from dawn to dusk. And on January 9, 1951, Mac-Arthur finally received a reply to his proposals of December 30 calling for four strong retaliatory measures against the Chinese.

The Joint Chiefs, with the President's approval, declined to allow the General to implement his proposals, although he was informed that they remained under consideration. Mac-Arthur was informed that "there is little possibility of policy change" and instructed to continue to defend successive positions and to inflict as much damage as possible on the Chinese. His primary considerations were the safety of his troops in Korea and the protection of Japan, and he was to withdraw to Japan if it became evident to him that evacuation was essential to avoid severe losses of men and matériel.

Instead of trying to follow these instructions, however unsatisfactory he might have thought they were, MacArthur, as he later wrote, "shot a query right back, asking for clarification in view of the self-evident fact that the strength of my command, as presently constituted, was insufficient to hold a position in Korea and simultaneously protect Japan against external assault."

In the course of a long and gloomy cable, the General stated that "Under the extraordinary limitations and conditions imposed upon the command in Korea . . . its military position is untenable, but it can hold, if overriding political considerations so dictate, for any length of time up to its complete destruction."

The limitations to which MacArthur referred were: "no reinforcements, no measures permissible against China's military potential, continued restrictions upon Chinese military action, and the concentration in the Korean-Manchurian sector of China's military force."

The Supreme Commander meant it when he told Ridgway on December 26 that the 8th Army was his and that he should do what he thought best. For after Ridgway's appearance, MacArthur appeared to lose interest in exercising close tactical supervision over military events in Korea. Instead, he largely devoted himself to a campaign of pressuring the Administration to adopt his policies for retaliation against the Chinese. This, of course, involved questions of foreign policy on the highest international level that were for the President to resolve, not a military commander, however illustrious he was or powerful his supporters in Congress.

MacArthur's cable of January 10 deeply disturbed the President and his advisers. As Truman later put it, "The Far East Commander was, in effect, reporting that the course of action decided by the National Security Council and by the Joint Chiefs of Staff and approved by me was not feasible."

The cordial relations between the President and the General apparent at Wake Island had deteriorated as the military situation in Korea worsened, and now, unknown to the public, they threatened to erupt into an open clash over policy. For the Administration had decided to localize the present conflict, even if this meant something less than conventional military victory. This decision was made primarily in the belief that throwing ever larger numbers of troops into Korea would weaken the American capacity to defend Western Europe and play into Communist hands. Widening the war would also lose support for the United States in the United Nations.

In contrast, MacArthur was determined to win in Korea, even though his proposals for doing so risked widening the war to mainland China and provoking a global war with the Soviet Union. The General was the first great commander to be handcuffed by the new concept of a limited war for limited goals, and he either did not understand this concept or understood it and refused to accept it. Accepting a stalemate, of course, would mean lesser glory for himself and an indecisive, even tarnished conclusion to a brilliant career.

For MacArthur, though he would never admit it, had committed blunders of monumental, even baffling, proportions. His "end-the-war" offensive did not provoke the Chinese attack of November 26. An assault on such a massive scale required preparation going back at least to the first crossings of the Yalu in mid-October.

Where the General blundered was in completely misreading Chinese intentions. He went ahead with his last offensive after the first two Chinese attacks revealed the plain evidence that the mountains of North Korea harbored an enemy force capable of destroying his command. He compounded this mistake by marching his forces right up toward the Manchurian border in divided formations that were fair game for just the kind of attack the Chinese were capable of launching and did launch. And as disastrous as were the results of these mistakes, MacArthur was wrong again in predicting the destruction of his command unless his proposals for vigorous retaliatory measures were accepted. Ridgway appeared to understand and to be capable of implementing the new strategy of holding the Chinese with the forces available to him.

The question at issue now, however, was not one of who had been right and who had been wrong. The President, his Secretary of State, and the Joint Chiefs had miscalculated Chinese intentions, too, and had acquiesced in MacArthur's bold strategy. They all displayed considerable hesitation, even seemed intimidated, in dealing with the prestigious Supreme Commander and could hardly accuse him of inviting disaster by violating a series of definite, clear-cut orders. The question now for the Administration was how to deal with a military commander who believed that its new policy was "not feasible."

The Administration's answer to this question was a series of patient attempts to make its thinking plain to MacArthur. The Joint Chiefs held consultations with State Department representatives on January 11 and 12, and on the latter date Truman convened a special meeting of the National Security

Council to discuss the United Nations Commander's pessimistic report. On January 12, the Joint Chiefs radioed MacArthur a new directive, which in essence repeated the instructions of January 9. The new directive read:

> We are forced to the conclusion, based upon all the factors known to us, including particularly those presented by you in your present message that it is infeasible under existing conditions, including sustained major effort by Communist China, to hold the position in Korea for a protracted period.
>
> It would be to our national interest, however, and also to the interest of the UN, before you issue firm instructions for initiation of evacuation of troops from Korea, to gain some further time for essential military and diplomatic consultations with UN countries participating in Korean effort.
>
> It is important also to future of UN and NATO organizations, to the United States prestige world-wide, and to efforts to organize anti-Communist resistance in Asia that maximum practicable punishment be inflicted on Communist aggressors and that Korea not be evacuated unless actually forced by military considerations.

At the National Security Council meeting, it was also decided that Truman should write a personal message to MacArthur "bringing him up to date on our foreign policy," according to the President. And on the evening of January 12, General Collins and General Vandenberg were sent to Tokyo by the President. This was done because Truman and the Joint Chiefs were concerned, as Collins put it, "that MacArthur should fully understand his new directive." According to Acheson, the President wanted the two generals "to report back on what the actual situation was, stripped of MacArthur's colorful rhetoric."

On January 14, Truman's long personal message to MacArthur arrived in Tokyo. It was an unusual and deferential communication, in tone almost as though the President were addressing another coequal head of state rather than a military commander.

"I want you to know," the telegram began, "that the situation in Korea is receiving the utmost attention here and that our efforts are concentrated upon finding the right decisions on this matter of the gravest importance to the future of America and to the survival of free peoples everywhere.

"I wish in this telegram to let you have my views as to our basic national and international purposes in continuing the resistance to aggression in Korea. . . ."

After pointing out that "Our course of action at this time should be such as to consolidate the great majority of the United Nations," the heart of the President's message read:

> We recognize, of course, that continued resistance might not be militarily possible with the limited forces with which you are being called upon to meet large Chinese armies. Further, in the present world situation, your forces must be preserved as an effective instrument for the defense of Japan and elsewhere. . . . In the worst case, it would be important that, if we must withdraw from Korea, it be clear to the world that the course is forced upon us by military necessity and that we shall not accept the result politically or militarily until the aggression has been rectified.

MacArthur interpreted this message to mean definitely that there would be no evacuation, and perhaps, in its reference to rectifying aggression, as an indication that the Administration might yet supply him with the military power to undertake more vigorous military action in Asia.

In any case, the concluding words of Truman's message were not likely to make MacArthur believe that the Administration was displeased either with his conduct of the war or his disagreements with its policies. "The entire nation," the President declared after the near-catastrophe that had taken place, "is grateful for your splendid leadership in the difficult struggle in Korea and for the superb performance of your forces under the most difficult circumstances."

On January 14, Collins and Vandenberg arrived in Tokyo and conferred with MacArthur. The Supreme Commander brought Truman's personal message to the conference room and opened the meeting by reading it to his visitors from

Washington. MacArthur said that he took the message as a directive to stay in Korea indefinitely. His forces could do this, but at the same time he could not assume responsibility for what might happen if Japan were left defenseless.

Collins attempted to explain that Truman's message was not a directive. What the President and his advisers had in mind was a flexible policy of delaying evacuation from Korea as long as possible without endangering Japan's security or that of the 8th Army. While maximum punishment was being inflicted upon the Chinese, the United Nations would be allowed time to find a political solution to the conflict.

The confusion over meanings was compounded when Collins read to MacArthur a memorandum prepared by the Joint Chiefs. It listed sixteen courses of action that might be taken if the U.N. forces were driven into a narrow defense perimeter with no hope of breaking out of it or if they were driven off the Korean Peninsula. Four of the sixteen possible courses of action were MacArthur's proposals for strong retaliation against the Chinese. The other twelve were military, economic, and diplomatic measures, such as increasing aid to Chiang Kai-shek and having Communist China labeled as an aggressor by the United Nations.

The sixteen points were not a directive or an official statement of policy, but simply a tentative memorandum that had not been approved by the President or the Secretaries of State or Defense. But MacArthur took the memorandum to mean that Washington was finally coming around to his view that strong measures against China should be and soon would be taken.

After the conference, Collins and Vandenberg flew to Korea. The Air Force Chief of Staff inspected Air Force units and installations and made an air and ground reconnaissance of the combat zone. Collins toured the front lines with Ridgway, who in some sectors had begun small counterattacks. What both members of the Joint Chiefs saw led them to believe that there was no imminent danger of the Chinese destroying the U.N. forces.

Upon returning to Tokyo on January 17, Collins radioed

General Bradley in the Pentagon, in part: "Eighth Army in good shape and improving daily under Ridgway's leadership. Morale very satisfactory considering conditions. ROK forces lack confidence and instinctively fear Chinese but are still capable of resistance against NK [North Korean] troops. No signs of disaffection or collapse though this could change quickly in event of serious reverses. . . . On the whole, Eighth Army now in position to punish severely any mass attack."

When Collins and Vandenberg arrived back in Washington on January 19 and made their full report, the Administration lost all interest in implementing the sixteen-point memorandum or taking any measures that would risk extending the war to mainland China. The great evacuation threat subsided because of what appeared to be a definite dwindling of Chinese offensive power.

The fact was that the Chinese were badly hurt. After their near-catastrophic rout of the U.N. forces in the far north, the Chinese found themselves in a far different situation while fighting 260 miles south of their supply bases near the Manchurian border. They were afflicted by hunger and outbreaks of typhus and the bitter cold. They were no better prepared for the continued freezing weather than the U.N. forces had initially been. Frostbite and trenchfoot took heavy tolls.

This military situation seemed to restore MacArthur's confidence. He visited Ridgway's headquarters on January 20 and told the correspondents assembled there: "There has been a lot of loose talk about the Chinese driving us into the sea, just as in the early days there was a lot of nonsense about the North Koreans driving us into the sea. No one is going to drive us into the sea. This command intends to maintain a military position in Korea just as long as Washington decides we should do so."

After speaking to the correspondents, MacArthur talked with Ridgway and ordered him "to start north again."

CHAPTER

FOURTEEN

The Dismissal

On February 1, the General Assembly of the United Nations passed an American resolution introduced on January 20 condemning China as an aggressor. Great Britain and France voted with the United States only after being assured that the latter would do everything possible to avoid expanding the war in Asia.*

However, other parts of the resolution indicated that the U.N. was still hoping for a cease-fire and was ready to accept one based on the prewar division of Korea. There was no recommendation to follow up the condemnation of Communist China with vigorous military action, a policy in which the United States concurred. This set the stage for further challenges by General MacArthur to President Truman and the United Nations.

MacArthur was now busy in Tokyo working out the final details of the Japanese peace treaty with John Foster Dulles. The Republicans' chief foreign policy strategist had arrived on his bipartisan mission on January 22 and remained in

---

* The vote was 40 to 7 for the resolution. India, Burma, and the Communist bloc voted against it, while the Arab-Asian bloc abstained.

Tokyo until February 9. In Korea, it became obvious that the Chinese, despite their Manchurian sanctuary and superior manpower, could not drive the U.N. off the peninsula and were not immune to defeat. MacArthur wanted to exploit this turn of events. He would not reconcile himself to limiting the conflict. The General likened the fighting back and forth at or near the 38th Parallel to the alternating rhythmic movement of an accordion. To him, nothing was settled by it, and the result was only endless destruction and the pointless loss of American lives.

On February 12, an influential congressman publicly voiced his support of MacArthur's views. In a speech in New York, Joseph Martin of Massachusetts, Republican Minority Leader in the House of Representatives, declared that the Democratic Administration was preventing eight hundred thousand Chinese Nationalists on Formosa from opening a "second front in Asia." Without explaining where he had obtained this exaggerated figure, Martin went on to say: "If we are not in Korea to win, then this Administration should be indicted for the murder of thousands of American boys."

Concerning the opening of a second front in Asia by Chiang Kai-shek, Martin said that: "There is good reason to believe that General MacArthur favors such an operation." In the Minority Leader's opinion, "the same State Department crowd that cut off aid" to Chiang in 1946 was resisting the use of his forces in 1951 because this would imply that they had been mistaken earlier.

Martin concluded his speech by declaring, in enthusiastic tones: "If we want a strategy that will save Europe and save Asia at the same time . . . we must clean out the State Department from top to bottom, starting with Dean Acheson."

Around this time, MacArthur began to formulate long-range plans "for destroying the Chinese forces in Korea." To seal off the Chinese in Korea from their supplies in Manchuria, he would have a five-mile-wide belt of radioactive cobalt spread below the Yalu River. Then he would make amphibious landings far up the east and west coasts, the landing parties to include Chiang Kai-shek's troops. "The Chinese would soon starve or surrender," the General reasoned. "Without food or ammunition they would become helpless. It would be something like Inchon, but on a much larger scale."

MacArthur, who never seemed to take into consideration the effect on world opinion of sowing atomic wastes across the Manchurian border, did not propose this strategy to the Administration at this time. Instead he flew to South Korea on February 20 to observe the launching of Operation Killer. Nine days earlier, the Chinese had begun their Fourth Phase Offensive. It had made some gains but had been contained after savage fighting. Operation Killer was the code name Ridgway had chosen for a counterattack operation he had planned and conceived. It was designed to kill as many Chinese as possible as the 8th Army ground its way back to the 38th Parallel. The apt code name of Operation Killer, however, caused General Collins to wince over its public relations connotations.

On the eve of the launch date, MacArthur stood before about ten correspondents at the X Corps Tactical Command Post, with Ridgway leaning against a table to the rear, and said calmly: "I have just ordered a resumption of the offensive." This announcement surprised and dismayed Ridgway. He knew that neither MacArthur nor his staff, although they had been informed in advance that it would take place, had had any role in conceiving or planning Operation Killer.

To Ridgway, this episode was "a rather unwelcome reminder of a MacArthur I had known but had almost forgotten," who tried to "keep his public image always glowing." The Supreme Commander also planned to be with the frontline troops at the actual beginning of the offensive. Ridgway dissuaded him from doing this on the grounds that it would alert the enemy that a major operation was coming.

Upon his return to Tokyo on February 21, MacArthur found another piece of frustrating news from Washington awaiting him. The Joint Chiefs turned down his request to bomb Racin. This port was an important Chinese Communist supply center in the northwest, only thirty-five miles below Soviet Siberia. Thus far Soviet Russia had made no moves to enter the Korean War, and had indeed made no moves to attack Western Europe. The Joint Chiefs did not want to take any action that would risk provoking the Russians.

On February 23, MacArthur complained in a report to the Joint Chiefs about the "unparalleled conditions of restraint and handicap" imposed on his command. Nevertheless, on March 1 the Joint Chiefs disapproved the request of the Far Eastern Air Force to bomb the generating plants along the Yalu River that were an important source of electrical power for Chinese Manchuria. In Korea, Operation Killer ground forward but achieved only moderate success. Thousands of Chinese were killed, but the bulk of their forces were able to escape wholesale slaughter because an early spring thaw and heavy rains turned the terrain into a quagmire that disrupted swift pursuit.

To MacArthur, the strategy of steady attrition exemplified by Operation Killer was not the solution to the problem of Chinese intervention in Korea in any case. Killing Chinese in Korea, no matter how many, would not stop Chinese aggression as long as Communist China's power to make war remained inviolate. By logical extension, MacArthur's strategy would have to involve destroying Chinese industry and killing Chinese soldiers in China itself.

Undaunted by the moderate success of Operation Killer, Ridgway pursued the strategy of attrition. He conceived Operation Ripper, whose objective was to kill Chinese and advance the United Nations line to within a few miles of the 38th Parallel. On March 7, the launch date of Operation Ripper, MacArthur flew to South Korea. To war correspondents gathered in a tent at Suwon Airfield he read from a penciled manuscript and noted that the progress of the campaign continued to be satisfactory.

However, the Supreme Commander pointed out, there should be no illusions in this matter. "Assuming no diminution of the enemy's flow of ground forces and matériel to the

Korean battle area," he declared in a grave, deliberate voice, "a continuation of the existing limitation upon our freedom of counteroffensive action, and no major additions to our organizational strength, the battle lines cannot fail in time to reach a point of theoretical military stalemate. Thereafter our further advance would militarily benefit the enemy more than it would ourselves."

The public hint here that MacArthur was dissatisfied with limitations that would lead to a stalemate could not have been more clear. In his concluding statement he said: "Vital decisions have yet to be made—decisions far beyond the scope of the authority vested in me as the military commander, decisions which are neither solely political nor solely military, but which must provide on the highest international levels an answer to the obscurities which now becloud the unsolved problems raised by Red China's undeclared war in Korea."

Upon his return to Tokyo on March 8, MacArthur found a letter waiting for him from Representative Martin. The House Minority leader wrote, in a vein that combined flattery with provocation:

> My dear General: In the current discussions on foreign policy and overall strategy many of us have been distressed that, although the European aspects have been heavily emphasized, we have been without the views of yourself as Commander in Chief of the Far Eastern Command.
>
> I think it is imperative to the security of our Nation and for the safety of the world that policies of the United States embrace the broadest possible strategy, and that in our earnest desire to protect Europe, we not weaken our position in Asia.
>
> Enclosed is a copy of an address I delivered in Brooklyn, N.Y., February 12, stressing this vital point and suggesting that the forces of Generalissimo Chiang Kai-shek on Formosa might be employed in the opening of a second Asiatic front to relieve the pressure on our forces in Korea.
>
> I have since repeated the essence of this thesis in other speeches, and intend to do so again on March 21, when I will be on a radio hookup.
>
> I would deem it a great help if I could have your views on

this point, either on a confidential basis or otherwise. Your admirers are legion, and the respect you command is enormous. May success be yours in the gigantic undertaking which you direct.

MacArthur, perhaps mindful of the presidential directive of December 6 that communications on national policy must first be cleared by the Defense and State Departments, did not reply to Martin's letter immediately. However, the Supreme Commander would eventually do so, with shattering consequences.

In Korea, General Ridgway called a press conference on March 12. The 8th Army commander wanted to counter the adverse effect on his forces' morale of MacArthur's implication five days earlier that American lives were being sacrificed for something less than victory.

"We didn't set out to conquer China," Ridgway told the press. "We set out to stop Communism. We have demonstrated the superiority on the battlefield of our men. If China fails to throw us into the sea, that is a defeat for her of incalculable proportions. If China fails to drive us from Korea, she will have failed monumentally. . . ."

Ridgway's opinion that reaching the 38th Parallel would constitute a victory was well received by the United Nations and the Administration, both of whom were about ready to adopt such a policy. The 8th Army commander's views, however, contrasted strikingly with those of MacArthur. While he continued to hold Ridgway in high regard as a military commander, the Supreme Commander later told correspondent Jim Lucas of the Scripps-Howard newspaper chain that Ridgway was a "chameleon" who agreed with MacArthur's plans until he found they were opposed by the Administration, after which came a "complete flipflop."

Operation Ripper reached the 38th Parallel. On March 15, Seoul changed hands for the fourth time. Entering the South Korean capital, Ridgway noticed that neither its lights nor streetcars worked and that its shopping district had been destroyed. He also saw about two hundred thousand "ragged, hungry, sick and scared" Koreans on hand to welcome his forces. The prewar population had been a million and a half.

Ridgway told himself that while Ripper, like Killer, had been successful in regaining ground, it had not been completely successful in its prime objective of destroying Chinese soldiers and their equipment. However, Ripper did bring the United Nations Command back to where it had been in October 1950 and presented the United Nations and the Administration with the necessity for making a decision. Should another drive beyond the 38th Parallel be undertaken?

On March 15, the day Seoul was retaken, MacArthur granted an interview to Hugh Baillie, president of United Press International. The General told Baillie that the U.N. could not stop on or near the 38th Parallel. He reasoned that there were no natural defenses in that area to hold against the Chinese; further maneuvering north was required. And indeed, as MacArthur spoke to Baillie, the General had received no new directive to cover the changed nature of the military situation. Privately, MacArthur felt that the Administration had "no policy . . . no plan or anything" for Korea.

However, the Administration was trying to formulate some kind of a plan in agreement with the other U.N. members participating in the war. On March 20, an agreement was reached, and the Joint Chiefs sent MacArthur the following message:

> State Department planning a Presidential announcement shortly that, with clearing bulk of South Korea of aggressors, United Nations now preparing to discuss conditions of settlement in Korea. United Nations feeling exists that further diplomatic efforts towards settlement should be made before any advance with major forces north of 38th Parallel. Time will be required to determine diplomatic reactions and permit new negotiations that may develop. Recognizing that parallel had no military significance, State has asked Joint Chiefs what authority you should have to permit sufficient freedom of action for next few weeks to provide security for United Nations forces and maintain contact with enemy. Your recommendations desired.

MacArthur replied to this message on March 21. His response was uncharacteristically mild, considering that the message constituted a rejection of his program and stated that a presidential announcement would soon be forthcoming aimed at a peace settlement. The General merely answered that his present directive was sufficient to cover the military situation, although he did not expect to be able to clear all of North Korea because of the limitations imposed upon him. Instead of calling for aggressive action, he only requested that "no further military restrictions be imposed upon the United Nations Command."

Nevertheless, that the intensity of MacArthur's frustration was increasing was indicated by his reply to Joe Martin's letter. The day before responding to the Joint Chiefs, the General wrote to the House Minority Leader:

Dear Congressman Martin: I am most grateful for your note of the 8th forwarding me a copy of your address of February 12. The latter I have read with much interest, and find that with the passage of years you have certainly lost none of your old-time punch.

My views and recommendations with respect to the situation created by Red China's entry into the war against us in Korea have been submitted to Washington in most complete detail. Generally these views are well known and clearly understood, as they follow the conventional pattern of meeting force with maximum counter-force, as we have never failed to do in the past. Your view with respect to the utilization of the Chinese forces on Formosa is in conflict with neither logic nor this tradition.

It seems strangely difficult for some to realize that here in Asia is where the Communist conspirators have elected to make their play for global conquest, and that we have joined the issue thus raised on the battlefield; that here we fight Europe's war with arms while the diplomats there still fight it with words; that if we lose this war to Communism in Asia the fall of Europe is inevitable; win it and Europe most probably would avoid war and yet preserve freedom. As you pointed out, we must win. There is no substitute for victory.

With renewed thanks and expressions of most cordial regard I am,

> Faithfully yours,
> Douglas MacArthur

The General attached little importance to this exchange of letters. To him it was just part of his routine practice in dealing with congressmen. Martin kept MacArthur's reply to himself at the time, so the Administration did not know that he had written it. The President, the Joint Chiefs, and the Secretaries of State and Defense were in any case busy completing the draft of the presidential announcement, which had the approval of other nations with troops in Korea.

Within the next few days, after South Korea was cleared of all remaining Chinese Communist troops, the President proposed to announce, in part, that a "prompt settlement of the Korean problem would greatly reduce international tension in the Far East and would open the way for the consideration of other problems in that area by the processes of peaceful settlement envisaged in the Charter of the United Nations."

What this planned presidential announcement amounted to was an open statement to the Chinese Communists and to the rest of the world that the United Nations and the United States were willing to negotiate a peace in Korea. The peace could be based on leaving Korea divided as it was before the North Koreans attacked south in June and before the United Nations drive to the Yalu. But Truman never made this statement. Before the President could do so, MacArthur made one of his own.

From Tokyo on March 24, the General issued a statement, without any prior consultation with the Administration, in which he spoke of the military weakness of "this new enemy, Red China, of such exaggerated and vaunted military power." MacArthur declared that the Chinese Communists were completely unable to conquer Korea, even given the restrictions under which the General's own forces were operating. "The enemy, therefore," MacArthur went on, "must by now be painfully aware that a decision of the United Nations to depart from its tolerant effort to contain the war to the area of Korea, through an expansion of our military operations to its coastal areas and interior bases, would doom Red China to the risk of imminent military collapse." In view of these basic facts, MacArthur said that he stood "ready at any time to confer in the field with the Commander-in-chief of the enemy forces in earnest effort to find any military means whereby realization of the political objectives of the United Nations in Korea, to which no nation may justly take exceptions, might be accomplished without further bloodshed."

Here was, in effect, a virtual ultimatum to Peking to admit that it had lost the battle along with an astonishing implied threat to expand the war to China's "coastal areas and interior bases" if the Chinese did not admit defeat. President Truman received the news of MacArthur's statement, according to Secretary Acheson, "in a state of mind that combined disbelief with controlled fury." It was, Truman has stated, "so entirely at cross purposes with the [announcement] I was to have delivered that it would only have confused the world if my carefully prepared statement had been made."

To Truman, MacArthur's act represented open defiance of the orders of the President and Commander-in-chief, a challenge to the authority of the President under the Constitution, and a flouting of the policy of the United Nations. Truman decided that he could no longer tolerate the Supreme Commander's insubordination. But, as had so often been the case with what he described as "my difficulties with MacArthur" since their Wake Island meeting, Truman took no direct action. He only instructed the Joint Chiefs to send to the General, on March 24, the following message:

> The President has directed that your attention be called to his order as transmitted 6 December 1950. In view of the information given you 20 March 1951 any further statements by you must be coordinated as prescribed in the order of 6 December.
>
> The President has also directed that in the event Communist

military leaders request an armistice in the field, you immediately report that fact to the JCS for instructions.

Truman wondered why MacArthur "was challenging the traditional civilian supremacy in our government" and found this latest development difficult to explain. He guessed that the General wanted to prevent anyone but himself from gaining credit for stopping the fighting. MacArthur himself considered his announcement as a routine communiqué, a "military appraisal," nothing more than a weapon of psychological warfare directed at the enemy. This explanation appears naive and less than adequate, but since it was the one MacArthur gave, any other explanations of his motives would always remain speculation.

Had the General lost all hope for the acceptance of his ideas and deliberately risked his career in order to thwart a negotiated settlement? Acting from what he considered the highest interests of the United States, did he try to appeal to the American people and his powerful supporters in Congress for more aggressive action against the Chinese over the heads of the Administration? Did he, in fact, desire to crush Communist China by extending the war to her mainland? The General himself denied this last speculation, declaring: "Anyone in favor of sending American ground troops to fight on Chinese soil should have his head examined." Nevertheless, MacArthur's March 24 announcement could not help but insure that Communist China's new and sensitive Government, representing one-quarter of humanity, would keep on fighting. How could Peking be sure which voice represented American foreign policy, the threatening statements of the Supreme Commander or the more conciliatory words of the Administration?

Whatever MacArthur's motives were for making what the Norwegian Ambassador to the United States termed his "pronunciamento," the immediate result of it was intense embarrassment for the Administration. The State Department was deluged with inquiries from its counterparts in other Western countries wondering if the United States was about to shift from its policy of attempting to make peace. That the Communist Chinese leaders continued to take, or pretended to take for propaganda purposes, MacArthur as a decisive voice in American foreign policy was indicated by a broadcast from Radio Peking: "Warmonger MacArthur made a fanatical but shameless statement with the intention of engineering the Anglo-American aggressors to extend the war of aggression into China. . . . MacArthur's shameless tricks . . . will meet with failure. . . . The people of China must raise their sense of vigilance by doubling their effort for the sacred struggle."

Incredibly, despite all that had just happened, the Administration forwarded no new instructions to the General telling him how far above the 38th Parallel his forces might now advance. On March 27, South Korean troops did cross the parallel again. On that date, Defense Secretary Marshall in Washington told the press corps that MacArthur was authorized to advance as far beyond the parallel as he considered necessary for military security. Marshall noted, however, that "Any general advance is a matter for political decision," which seemed to indicate that enthusiasm for another drive to the Yalu had abated.

On March 31, MacArthur reported to the Joint Chiefs that another full-scale Chinese offensive could be expected at any time in April. On April 3, the General flew to Korea to confer with Ridgway. The latter's new Operation Rugged had brought South Korean, and now American troops as well, to a line about six to eight miles north of the parallel. MacArthur told Ridgway that any further advance at this time should be carefully controlled and limited. The Supreme Commander was still very much in charge of the unfolding events, and it appeared that the furor caused by his announcement of March 24 had blown over. Then, on April 5, Joe Martin rose on the floor of the House of Representatives and declared that he "owed it to the American people to tell them the information I had from a great and reliable source."

The Republican Minority Leader, a long-time isolationist

and vociferous foe of Democratic administrations, then proceeded to read MacArthur's reply to his letter of March 8. MacArthur later said that Martin took this step for reasons unknown and without consulting him. The General, however, had given no indication that he wanted the contents of the letter withheld.

When he learned of Martin's reading of MacArthur's letter, President Truman told himself that the "time had come to draw the line." He was particularly disturbed by the General's comment that it was in Asia that the Communists had elected "to make their play for global conquest." To the President, the Communists were just as capable of attacking in Europe. This was why he did not want to extend the conflict in Korea. On Friday morning, April 6, he called Acheson, Bradley, Marshall, and Averell Harriman into his office and asked them what should be done about MacArthur.

During a discussion that lasted about an hour, Harriman told the President that he should have fired the General two years before. Marshall advised caution and asked for time to reflect further. The Secretary of Defense observed that if Truman relieved MacArthur it might cause difficulties in getting military appropriations through Congress. Bradley thought that MacArthur's was a clear case of insubordination and that he deserved to be relieved in the interests of military discipline. However, the Chairman of the Joint Chiefs of Staff preferred not to make a final recommendation until he could consult with the other three members of that body, who were out of town. Acheson was of the opinion that the situation created by MacArthur's open defiance of the President could only be resolved by relieving the General from all of his many commands and removing him from the Far East. The Secretary of State, however, counseled that the President should have the unanimous support of his civilian and military advisers before he acted. "If you relieve MacArthur," Acheson added, "you will have the biggest fight of your administration."

Truman said nothing about what he intended to do, and this meeting ended with no decision having been reached.

Those participating in it went to a regularly scheduled Cabinet meeting, where the question of what to do about the General was not discussed. This was resumed after the Cabinet meeting when Acheson, Marshall, Bradley, and Harriman reconvened in Truman's office. Again no decision was reached. The President asked Marshall to study all of the messages in the Pentagon files that had been exchanged with MacArthur in the past two years and return with the rest of the group the following morning at 9 A.M.

This next meeting was short. During it, Marshall said that after studying the files he had come to the conclusion that MacArthur should have been relieved two years ago. Truman asked Bradley to consult with the other members of the Joint Chiefs on Sunday and make a final recommendation to him on Monday. Bradley did this, while Truman again conferred with Acheson.

At 9 A.M. on Monday, April 9, Marshall, Bradley, Harriman, and Acheson met with the President in his office. Speaking for Generals Collins and Vandenberg and Admiral Sherman, Bradley declared that it was the unanimous recommendation of the Joint Chiefs that MacArthur should be relieved. Harriman, Marshall, and Acheson agreed. It was only then that Truman told them that he had already made up his mind that MacArthur must go after the General's announcement of March 24. The Martin episode was only the culmination of a long series of provocations.

All that remained now was for orders to be prepared and transmitted to the General informing him that he was relieved of all of his commands. It was decided that the orders should be delivered personally by Secretary of the Army Frank Pace, who was in Korea. Meanwhile, steps were taken to inform important members of Congress and foreign officials, such as Prime Minister Shigeru Yoshida of Japan, what was coming.

On Wednesday, April 11, General MacArthur and his wife Jean were entertaining William Sterns of Northwest Airlines and Senator Warren Magnuson of Washington at luncheon in the American Embassy in Tokyo. After finishing luncheon, the General intended to fly to the front in Korea. But his wife was called from the table to take a telephone call from Colonel Sidney Huff, MacArthur's aide-de-camp. Huff said that he had just heard a special radio bulletin from Washington, which had preempted the regular programming. "President Truman," the bulletin said, "has just removed General MacArthur from his Far Eastern and Korean Commands and from the occupation of Japan." No reason was given for the President's action, beyond a doubt that MacArthur was able to "support the policies of the Administration."

Mrs. MacArthur went over to her husband and told him quietly what Colonel Huff had heard on the radio. The General betrayed no emotion. To his wife he said: "Jeannie, we're going home at last." Thus, by means of a public radio broadcast, did General of the Army Douglas MacArthur, Supreme Commander, Allied Powers, Japan; Commander-in-chief, United Nations Command; and Commander-in-chief, Far East, learn that his military career of fifty-two years was over.

"No office boy, no charwoman, no servant of any sort would have been dismissed with such callous disregard for the ordinary decencies," MacArthur later wrote about what he described as "my abrupt relief when victory was within my grasp." The way in which he learned of his relief, however, was owing to a communications mix-up rather than to the President's desire to humiliate a proud and sensitive man. Something went wrong with the commercial cable line that was to transmit the coded orders to Secretary Pace. Fearing a press leak before Pace could be contacted, Truman decided to make the announcement at a special news conference hurriedly called for 1 A.M., April 11.

At this conference, Truman explained that he was relieving MacArthur because the General "is unable to give his whole-hearted support to the policies of the United States Government and of the United Nations in matters pertaining to his official duties." The relief orders were then on their way to

Tokyo through the Army's own cable system, but arrived after the news of the President's press conference had been broadcast over the public radio.

Ridgway had been appointed to take over all of Mac-Arthur's commands. The 8th Army commander, who was to be replaced in that post by General James Van Fleet, flew from Korea to Tokyo on April 12. Ridgway had a natural human curiosity about what MacArthur's reaction would be to his discharge. He found the General to be "composed, quiet, temperate, friendly, and helpful to the man who was to succeed him," and without anger or bitterness.

MacArthur then prepared to return to the United States. He could not know what kind of reception awaited him in a country he had not seen for fourteen years. He was, after all, now only a professional soldier whose career was finished. But MacArthur's career as a major factor in American politics, and by extension world affairs, was far from finished. Harry Truman, as Dean Acheson had predicted, was about to have "the biggest fight of his administration on his hands."

CHAPTER FIFTEEN

The Hero Returns

President Truman was hanged and burned in effigy in San Gabriel, California, on April 12. This was only one manifestation of the bewilderment, anger, and shock that greeted the news of MacArthur's relief. Its graceless, inept handling partly accounted for this reaction. It was also owing to the fact that the American people, and most of their elected representatives, had not been prepared for the sudden dismissal in any way. The country had been taken into a major undeclared war by presidential decision and without congressional consent. That war was going badly, and now the Administration had fired an authentic military hero who still spoke confidently of victory.

The President and his advisers had sound reasons for their decision. But it had been taken in secret, as had all the major decisions relating to the Korean War. The American people simply did not know in any detail how the present murderous stalemate had come about or why MacArthur had been fired. The result was an emotional outpouring of frustration and rage unprecedented in American history and a disbelief in the Government. The Administration seems not to have anticipated how strong this reaction would be.

179

In Pasadena on April 12, Lewis Gough, national vice-commander of the American Legion, said: "I know the amazing news of the removal of one of the greatest military leaders of all time will stun and shock the 4,000,000 members of the American Legion and its auxiliary." The Los Angeles City Council adjourned "in sorrowful contemplation of the political assassination" of General MacArthur, and he was cabled to accept the hospitality of San Francisco by its mayor, Elmer Robinson.

In Lafayette, Indiana, employees of Consolidated Industries quit work. Carrying signs reading "We Want Mac Back" and "Out H.S.T.," they paraded to the local telegraph office and sent messages of complaint to Washington. Two thousand longshoremen walked off the Chelsea piers along the North River in New York City to stage a protest demonstration in a nearby park. Members of the Irish Minute Men of 1949 picketed the British Consulate in the Empire State Building, carrying such signs as "England Communism Acheson Fired MacArthur."

Before addressing the Wisconsin Furniture Dealers Association in Milwaukee, Senator Joe McCarthy said that President Truman must have been drunk on "bourbon and benedictine" when he made his decision and described him as a "sonofabitch" who should be impeached. In his speech to the furniture dealers, McCarthy demanded that the American people fight the General's ouster lest "Red waters lap at our shores."

In Washington, Representative George Bender, Republican of Ohio, complained that the dismissal had cost him fifteen dollars. "I got about sixty telegrams at my hotel from outraged constituents," Bender said. "Every time a bell-boy brought one up, I had to tip him a quarter." On the floor of the Senate, William Jenner, Republican of Indiana, declared that "this country today is in the hands of a secret inner coterie which is directed by agents of the Soviet Union. We must cut this whole cancerous conspiracy out of our Government at once. Our own choice is to impeach President Truman and find out who is the secret invisible government which has so cleverly led our country down the road to destruction."

Some of the major figures of the Republican Party, which had been out of national power for nineteen years, gathered in the office of Joe Martin. They included Floor Leader Kenneth Wherry and Senator Taft. Emerging from the conference, Martin told reporters that it had been agreed that there should be an investigation of the Administration's military and foreign policy "in the light of the latest tragic development," and that MacArthur should be invited to express his views before Congress. Furthermore, Martin said that "the question of possible impeachments was discussed," although he did not specify which individuals he meant.

Senator Taft issued no formal statement after the conference beyond expressing his regret that America was "losing a great general." Taft was not given to making inflammatory statements, but his reserve perhaps had another cause. He was the leading candidate for the Republican presidential nomination in 1952. While it was one thing to offer MacArthur unqualified support while he was in the Far East, it was another to do so now that he was a possible candidate himself. In any case, it was impossible to determine at this time whether the Republican leaders had simply seized upon the MacArthur issue as a convenient stick with which to beat the Democrats or whether they were serious about supporting his Far Eastern policies. What was certain was that no prominent Democrat dared to brave the current furor by publicly defending the President and his Secretary of State. They could only, in Acheson's opinion, settle down to "endure the heavy shelling from press and Congress," meanwhile preparing the release of some documents that attempted to explain their side of the case.

However, there was relief at the news of MacArthur's dismissal in European government circles. His disagreements with the Administration's policy of priority for Europe over Asia were well known, and his attitude was regarded as one likely to increase the risk of general war. In Tokyo, the General himself issued no provocative statements and seemed calm as he prepared to return to the United States at the height of a gathering partisan storm.

On April 15, Emperor Hirohito paid a farewell visit to the deposed Supreme Commander at his residence in the American Embassy. This was regarded as a tremendous honor by the Japanese, for it was the first time in their history that a Japanese Emperor had left his palace to call on a foreign citizen who held no official position.

Prime Minister Yoshida also honored the departing proconsul with a radio broadcast in which he said: "The accomplishments of General MacArthur in the interest of our country are one of the marvels of history. It is he who has salvaged our nation from post-surrender confusion and prostration, and steered the country on the road of recovery and reconstruction. . . . I have no words to convey the regret of our nation to see him leave."

In the chill dawn of April 16, MacArthur left his residence in the American Embassy for the last time. He got into his black limousine with his wife Jean and their son Arthur. The thirteen-year-old boy had never been in the United States and had been tutored privately in Japan by an English governess. The General was driven to the airport past solid files of Japanese police and a crowd, some of whose members were waving and some weeping, which he remembered as numbering two million and which the Tokyo police estimated at two hundred and thirty thousand.

After a nineteen-gun salute at the airport and another salute by a flight of eighteen jet fighters and four Superfortress bombers, MacArthur's personal silver Constellation flew west. Once the *SCAP* (Supreme Commander, Allied Powers), the plane had just been renamed *Bataan*. It sped across the International Dateline and came to rest first in Hawaii. A crowd of about one hundred thousand cheered the General in warm tropic sunshine along a twenty-mile parade route from the airport to Honolulu. There he was awarded the honorary degree of Doctor of Civil Laws by the University of Hawaii, and he laid a wreath at the National Memorial Cemetery of the Pacific. Then the *Bataan* was off for San Francisco, touching down at 8:29 P.M., April 17.

The police were unable to contain the people pushing against the barriers at International Airport, many of whom broke through to touch or shake the returning General's hand. Smiling and waving, he rode past cheering crowds to the Saint Francis Hotel. The trip normally took thirty minutes, but this one took nearly two hours because of massive traffic jams. The next morning MacArthur was cheered during a two-hour ticker-tape parade through San Francisco's business and financial district. Some of the guests at the Saint Francis showered him with feathers obtained by tearing up their pillows. For this gesture, the hotel management charged them fifteen dollars per pillow. The *Bataan* left San Francisco early in the afternoon and landed in Washington shortly after midnight of April 19.

A crowd of twelve thousand at the airport greeted the General with "an almost hysterical welcome," according to one newspaper account. Some of the three hundred photographers and reporters detailed to cover the event prepared for trouble by wearing football helmets. Major General Harry Vaughan, the President's personal representative, the Joint Chiefs of Staff, and Defense Secretary Marshall could only offer a brief welcome before being swept aside by a surging crowd that encircled the *Bataan* and obliged MacArthur to fight his way to his waiting limousine. The following day, as he had been invited to do, he would address Congress.

Those in the crowded public galleries and the members of the Senate and House rose and applauded as the General appeared at 12:31, walked down the aisle, and took his place on the rostrum before a battery of microphones. An estimated 20 million Americans were watching and listening on television, a relatively new medium. RCA Victor had placed advertisements tempting people to buy one of its television sets on the ground that they could witness "the greatest single dramatic news event of the generation," for which a "whole nation, indeed an entire world, stands poised in anticipation."

General MacArthur was more than up to the occasion. In a speech of thirty-seven minutes, delivered in a forceful, unhurried, dramatic voice, he put forth his side of the case, noting that "I address you with neither rancor nor bitterness in the fading twilight of life with but one purpose in mind, to serve my country." As for China, he said that "I have from the beginning believed that the Chinese Communists' support of the North Koreans was the dominant one." The General did not bother to explain why he had advised the President at Wake Island that there was very little possibility of the Chinese entering the war or why he had driven on to the Yalu after clear evidence of their entry in October. Now he said that "no man in his right mind would advocate sending our ground forces into continental China," but recommended:

1. The intensification of our economic blockade against China;
2. The imposition of a naval blockade against the China coast;
3. Removal of restrictions on air reconnaissance of China's coastal area and of Manchuria;
4. Removal of restrictions on the forces of the Republic of China on Formosa with logistic support to contribute to their effective operations against the common enemy.

MacArthur denied that he was a warmonger, noting that "I know war as few other men now living know it, and nothing to me is more revolting." But, he continued, "once war is forced upon us, there is no other alternative than to apply every available means to bring it to a swift end. War's very object is victory—not prolonged indecision. In war, indeed, there can be no substitute for victory."

The General then came to the climax of his speech. Though his critics might find it melodramatic or even corny, there was no doubt that its sheer emotional impact had rarely been equaled in American history.

"I am closing my fifty-two years of military service. When I joined the Army even before the turn of the century, it was the fulfillment of all my boyish hopes and dreams. The world has turned over many times since I took the oath on the Plain at West Point, and the hopes and dreams have long since vanished. But I still remember the refrain of one of the most popular barrack ballads of that day which proclaimed most proudly that—

'Old soldiers never die, they just fade away.'

"And like the old soldier of that ballad, I now close my military career and just fade away—an old soldier who tried to do his duty as God gave him the light to see that duty.

"Good-by."

The reaction of one Congressman, Representative Dewey Short of Missouri, to MacArthur's speech was: "We saw a great hunk of God in the flesh, and we heard the voice of God." Representative Short had been educated at Harvard, Oxford, and Heidelberg. To Herbert Hoover, MacArthur was the "reincarnation of Saint Paul into a great General of the Army who came out of the East." Not everyone was as impressed as the former President by the General's speech. Dean Acheson, for one, hoped that MacArthur would now fade away. But unfortunately for the Administration the hope of the Secretary of State was not to be fulfilled.

After his speech to Congress, the General drove in a motorcade down Pennsylvania Avenue as a quarter of a million Washingtonians cheered and jet fighters and bombers roared overhead. Then he flew to New York, where he and his party checked into the Waldorf-Astoria Hotel. America's largest city was to honor him with a parade the next day.

Friday, April 20, was a warm day of brilliant sunshine, cloudless blue skies, and a slight wind. At 11:05, the General left the East Forty-ninth Street exit of the Waldorf-Astoria and got into a long, open car also seating Grover Whalen, chairman of the Mayor's Reception Committee, and Mayor Vincent Impellitteri. Mrs. MacArthur and Arthur, their son, entered another car. Crowds jammed behind wooden police barricades cheered the appearance of the General. The press of people was so dense that two other residents of the hotel, the Duke and Duchess of Windsor, were obliged to walk in the middle of the street in order to reach a friend's apartment three blocks north on Park Avenue, where they were to watch the motorcade.

Led by an honor escort of police motorcycles, four abreast and with red lights flashing, the General's motorcade moved up Park Avenue and entered Central Park. Children from public, private, and parochial schools lined the park's east and west drives. One group of cheering students from Cardinal Hayes High School held aloft a large banner reading: "Welcome Back—God Bless You, Mac."

As the motorcade left the Central Park South exit at 11:50 A.M. and moved down Broadway, General MacArthur could see that he was the subject of a triumphant procession that had been accorded no other man since New York was incorporated as New Amsterdam in 1653. A cascade of torn paper billowed down from office and apartment building windows and covered the General's gold-braided cap. The spring snowstorm of paper at times hid MacArthur from the view of those hoping for a glimpse of the returning hero.

The Sanitation Department estimated that 2,850 tons of ticker tape, confetti, and other paper were thrown along the nineteen-mile parade route. The tonnage was heavier than that for the next three leading New York City parade figures, Howard Hughes in 1938, Charles Lindbergh in 1927, and Douglas (Wrong-Way) Corrigan in 1938. Faced with cleaning up the debris, Sanitation Commissioner Andrew Mulrain remarked: "This is going to be a tough job, but it's well worth it!"

Hawkers moved through the Broadway area pushing corncob pipes and buttons reading: "Welcome Back Mac," and "MacArthur for President." Sales in the city's retail stores were almost brought to a halt. This was especially true along Fifth Avenue, where Plummer, Limited, had on sale for $10.50 a seven-inch-high "General MacArthur Toby Jug, perfectly executed as to coloring and uniform. A great likeness of a great soldier."

Seven thousand policemen, almost half of the city's total

force, were hard pressed to control the cheering, surging crowds, estimated at seven and a half million. This was nearly twice as many people as had welcomed General Eisenhower upon his return from Europe in 1945. The only serious incident occurred when Mario Riccobono, a forty-seven-year-old man from Queens, was hit on the head by a five-pound metal paperweight tossed or dropped from a window of the Woolworth Building. Riccobono was rushed to the hospital with a possible fractured skull.

At noon, the motorcade turned left at Thirty-fourth Street, entered the Franklin D. Roosevelt Drive, and sped toward lower Manhattan. As he was driven along the East River, the General's ears were struck by tugboat blasts and ships' whistles, and he saw water sprays, from three city tugboats, swirling gracefully in the blue sky. Twenty-five minutes later, the traditional ticker-tape parade up Lower Broadway to City Hall got under way. To acknowledge the thunderous acclaim and another storm of swirling white paper, the General raised his right arm and waved his gloved right hand. Secret Service men trotted on either side of his open car and jumped on its running boards when, infrequently, it was able to pick up speed.

In City Hall, Mayor Impellitteri presented MacArthur with New York's official scroll for distinguished service and the city's gold medal of honor. Then the triumphant motorcade moved north again. One spectator, William Styron, heard what he felt was the "avid buzz of patriotic hysteria." Styron, a Marine Corps lieutenant in World War II, had been recalled to active duty and was about to report to the Second Marine Division in North Carolina.

As he watched the passing motorcade on Fifth Avenue, Styron saw MacArthur looking straight at him. The young Marine, later to become a Pulitzer Prize winning novelist, thought that the General's eyes were "like those of a man whose thoughts had turned inward upon some Caesarean dream magnificent beyond compare." Hearing a nearby voice cry: "Hang that bastard Harry Truman!" Styron stifled the urge to hit somebody.

At 2:30, the motorcade reached Saint Patrick's Cathedral. There, Archbishop Spellman rose from his cardinal's chair placed at the top of the cathedral's front steps. He walked down the steps and warmly greeted his old friend, as police struggled to hold back frantically cheering spectators, as well as reporters and newsmen.

At six minutes past three, an hour behind schedule, Mac-Arthur was back at the Waldorf-Astoria to attend a civic luncheon given in his honor at the Starlight Roof. When it was over, Grover Whalen turned to the General and said: "I'm sure if all of us could just fade away, the way the General faded away today . . ." Whalen could not finish because of the loud applause. MacArthur then gave a short farewell speech to the eight hundred guests and the millions listening on radio, in which he said: "You have done what an enemy in the last ten years in savage campaigns in the Pacific has been unable to do. You have forced us to capitulate. At long last we do surrender."

The General then left the Starlight Roof's dais, behind which was a large shield bearing his five-star insignia and the Great Seal of the United States, as a string ensemble played "Old Soldiers Never Die." Looking somewhat tired now, he went to his thirty-seventh-floor presidential suite to rest. This day of triumph was over for him, but more were to come.

On the same afternoon that MacArthur was receiving this unprecedented accolade in New York, President Truman went to Griffith Stadium in Washington to throw out the traditional first ball in the opening game of the baseball season between the Washington Senators and the New York Yankees. Entering the park to the strains of "Hail to the Chief," Truman was greeted with light, scattered applause mixed with boos. It was the first time a President had been booed in a baseball stadium since Herbert Hoover received similar greetings when throwing out the first ball of the 1931 World Series in Philadelphia. Truman was again booed, this time lustily, when he left Griffith Stadium after the top of the ninth inning. The Yankee's well-publicized rookie, Mickey Mantle, had then hit a triple, but it was not enough to keep the Senators from winning the game, 5 to 3.

In Cairo on the same April 20, Trygve Lie, Secretary General of the United Nations, was asked whether the removal of General MacArthur had improved the chances for peace in Korea. Lie reported that he thought that the outlook for a settlement was now better. A special correspondent of *The New York Times* reported from Melbourne that "Australian opinion is flatly opposed to the strategy recommended by General of the Army Douglas MacArthur in his address to Congress on the ground that it would inevitably provoke a large-scale war with Communist China and possibly the Soviet Union also and have an appalling effect on the Asiatic peoples generally."

In Korea itself, Chinese units continued to withdraw above the 38th Parallel, but some of their rear guards suddenly turned and fought 8th Army formations. General Ridgway and the new 8th Army commander, General Van Fleet, now wondered whether the Chinese were withdrawing in order to lure their adversaries into another trap or whether they were regrouping for another major offensive to the south despite their heavy losses. The Department of the Army estimated enemy casualties thus far as 813,873, broken down to 291,895 Chinese and 504,835 North Korean. Another body count of 17,143 had not been identified as being Chinese or North Korean. As of April 18, United States casualties were 9,195 killed, 40,681 wounded, and 10,899 missing, for a total of 60,775.

As the war continued its indecisive course and American casualties continued to mount with no end in sight, prominent Republicans intensified their demands for a full-scale investigation of the Administration's conduct of affairs in Korea and the Far East. In Washington on April 22, Senator Nixon of California said that only full disclosure of all relevant material would satisfy Congress. "Certainly," he declared, "if classified documents are now to be made public the committees of Congress and the American people should be entitled to see not only those documents which might reflect against MacArthur, but also those which might reflect in his favor." Senator Nixon asserted that "one of the most vicious smear campaigns in history" was being planned against MacArthur and that "the smear brigade and professional lint pickers" were working around the clock.

The "first salvo" in this smear campaign, Nixon declared, had been fired the day before "with the publication in *The New York Times* of secret documents covering the Wake Island meeting between the President and General MacArthur, obviously selected to spotlight every action of the general which might reflect on him unfavorably." The junior Senator from California concluded his remarks by saying that the Democratic Administration might better spend its time and energy "devising ways to develop an effective Far Eastern diplomatic and military policy and thereby bring to an end the appalling casualties in Korea."

The Times had, in fact, published documents on the October 15 meeting in the Pacific obtained by one of its Washington correspondents, Anthony Leviero. However, despite Nixon's assertion, the documentation appeared to be complete and not selected to put MacArthur in a bad light. The General himself never disputed its accuracy.

Leviero's story pointed out that MacArthur had told the President that he thought there was very little possibility of Chinese intervention and predicted that organized resistance to the United Nations would end throughout Korea by Thanksgiving. This was the first inkling that the general public and most members of Congress had that MacArthur was not always right in his military forecasts or judgments about what the leaders of Oriental countries would do. Nevertheless, there was no letup in the Republican assault upon the Truman Administration over the issue of the General's dismissal and the situation in Korea. Senator Nixon declared that "The new test for classifying secret documents now seems to be not whether the publication of a document would affect the secur-

ity of the nation, but whether it would affect the political security of the Administration."

While Nixon was making his charges, two other influential
Republicans attacked Dean Acheson. The senior Senator from
California, William Knowland, declared that there would be
"great difficulty" in getting Republicans and Democrats together on the best way to conduct the Korean War as long as
Acheson was Secretary of State. Joe McCarthy said, "Acheson
has become President and the State Department is going to run
the military and everything else." From a nongovernment
source came another complaint. Addressing the Florida State
Legion convention in Tampa, Erle Cocke, Jr., National Commander of the American Legion, asserted to ringing applause
that "Military decisions must govern the methods and tactics
of defeating the enemy. This is no job for swivel-chair politi-
cians or striped-pants diplomats. This is a job for soldiers.
Soldiers have always fought our wars, and they should fight
this war and the wars of the future."

The Republican demand for a full-scale senatorial investigation could not be avoided. An inquiry was agreed to, conducted jointly by the Foreign Relations Committee and the
Armed Services Committee. As chairman of the latter committee, Senator Richard Russell, Democrat of Georgia, would
preside. However, Russell noted that the continuing round of
welcomes for MacArthur might well delay the start of the
inquiry. Russell allowed that the General was free to attend
all the festivities he wished but observed dryly that "of course
if he has embarked on a grand tour of the country, that might
put a new complexion on the matter."

MacArthur did seem to be taking part in a grand tour, although General Whitney preferred to call it "a crusade to
revitalize the nation." Meanwhile, in Korea, savage fighting
resumed. Under a full moon just before midnight of April 22,
the Chinese launched their "First Impulse, Fifth Phase Offensive." As smudge from thousands of brush fires partially neu-
tralized United Nations air intervention the next morning,

Chinese infantry drove south in wave after calculated wave.

The Chinese High Command seemed, in desperation, to have decided to overcome the United Nations weapons superiority by saturating the enemy with sheer humanity. The strategy failed, as the attackers were shredded in the U.N. meat grinder. On April 29, after making gains in some places of thirty-five miles but taking around seventy thousand casualties, the Chinese fell back to reorganize and reequip for the "Second Impulse, Fifth Phase Offensive."

In the United States, General MacArthur continued his crusade. On April 26, he flew to Chicago and was met there by Mayor Martin Kennelly and the Governor of Illinois, Adlai Stevenson. Some two million Chicagoans cheered the General as his motorcade moved slowly from O'Hare Field down State Street and on to the Stevens Hotel on the lakefront. Along the route, he could see waving banners that read: "We're With You Mac" and "God Bless Mac Our Next President."

That evening fifty-five thousand people jammed into Soldier Field and heard MacArthur declare: "I have endeavored since my return home to keep the issue on a higher level than partisan politics. The lives of your sons call for this measure of consideration. For the enemy bullets have no respect for political affiliation and strike down the son of the Democrat just as surely as the son of a Republican. Although my public life is now closed and I no longer carry any responsibilities of the national administration, I feel my responsibility of national citizenship no less deeply." The General's reference to his public life now being closed provoked a roar of protest from the crowd in the stadium. A tumult of applause greeted his contention that a realistic American policy in Korea must replace the present "policy vacuum heretofore unknown to war."

The next day, MacArthur went to Milwaukee, where he had spent one and a half years of his boyhood but which he had last seen while attending his father's funeral in 1912. Returning thirty-nine years later, the General was awarded an honorary doctor of laws by Marquette University and was wildly cheered while touring MacArthur Square in downtown Milwaukee.

Why were the unprecedented crowds cheering? What accounted for the tremendous reception that MacArthur received wherever he appeared—on the East or West Coasts or in the heartland of the Middle West? It was a question that President Truman might well ponder, and Mao Tse-tung as well. For MacArthur was being welcomed as a conquering hero rather than as a discredited general, and he appeared to be the most popular man in America.

Was the frenzied, and at times semihysterical, enthusiasm for him simply a response to MacArthur's oratorical and dramatic powers, soldierly bearing, and photogenic personality? Were the crowds only giving vent to the most basic kind of unreasoning patriotism and welcoming home after a fourteen-year absence an authentic military hero in a frustrating period of Cold War in which authentic heroes were scarce?

Or did something deeper lie behind the response to the General? He had challenged and criticized the President of the United States in a public speech to Congress. The speech seemed to increase, rather than diminish, his popularity. Was a basic tenet of American democracy, that the military was subordinate to elected civilian officials, in danger of being ruptured? Were the American people, baffled and frustrated by a new kind of war that the United States did not seem to be able to either win or end, ready to follow a general who held out the promise of a solution? Could MacArthur, with his powerful supporters in Congress and tremendous public backing, force the Administration to adopt his more aggressive policies toward Communist China? Could the General translate his public popularity and congressional support into the winning of the Republican nomination and election to the presidency of the United States in 1952?

An attempt to answer more specific questions, such as the reasons for MacArthur's abrupt dismissal and the wisdom of the Administration's Far Eastern policy, would be made at the forthcoming full-scale congressional investigation. When the cheering for the General stopped temporarily, the inquiry began, on Thursday morning, May 3, in Room 318 of the Senate Office Building. This was the Caucus Room, with marble columns and high ceilings, where all major Senate investigations were conducted.

The general public, as well as radio, newspaper, and television reporters, was barred from the Caucus Room for reasons of military security. However, transcripts of the testimony taken were given to reporters at the end of the day after sensitive military information was deleted by a group of Defense Department censors headed by Vice-Admiral Arthur Davis.

The first witness to be sworn in was MacArthur. He took his place on the stand around 10:30 A.M., dressed in a battle jacket that bore no decorations except for the five small stars of a General of the Army. MacArthur did not think much of these hearings. His attitude was that he had already made his position clear in his address to Congress. "I appear today," he told the committee members, "not as a voluntary witness at all but in response to the request of the committee, and I am entirely in the hands of the committee."

MacArthur remained on the stand for three days, for a total of twenty-one hours and ten minutes. Each morning he flew to Washington from New York in the *Bataan* and then returned to his $130-a-day suite in the Waldorf-Astoria after testifying. Twelve other witnesses were questioned, including Secretary of State Acheson, Secretary of Defense Marshall, and the Joint Chiefs of Staff. The witnesses submitted to forty-three days of questioning, during which more than two million words of testimony were taken. The printed record, entitled *Military Situation in the Far East,* totaled 3691 pages including appendices. While the hearings were going on, the Chinese launched their "Second Impulse, Fifth Phase Offensive" on May 16. It was effectively halted four days later.

As the first witness, MacArthur was persuasive and cooperative. At no point did he question the President's right to dis-

miss him but still thought that victory was not the purpose
of the Administration, only to "go on indecisively, fighting with
no mission for the troops except to resist and fight in this
accordion fashion—up and down—which means that your
cumulative losses are going to be staggering." He was of the
opinion that his views on achieving military victory were "fully
shared" by the Joint Chiefs of Staff and referred to their recommendations of January 12. These recommendations, Mac-
Arthur thought, must have been vetoed by the President or
Secretary of Defense Marshall. Although he treated the General with deference, as did all of the other questioners, a
freshman Senator from Texas, Lyndon Johnson, wanted to
know more about this matter.

"Has there been any other indication other than the documents of January the twelfth to the effect that the Joint Chiefs
support the program you advocate?" Johnson asked.

"Nothing in the writing that I know of," MacArthur replied.

"Anything orally?"

"Nothing that I know of."

As it turned out, all four members of the Joint Chiefs did
not support MacArthur's program, had supported the President in relieving him, and agreed with the Administration in
its efforts to prevent the Korean War from expanding into a
conflict with China or Russia, or both. Speaking for the Joint
Chiefs, their chairman, General Bradley, summarized their
differences with MacArthur in one statement:

> Korea, in spite of the importance of the engagement, must
> be looked upon with proper perspective. It is just one engage-
> ment, just one phase of this battle. . . .
>
> As long as we keep the conflict within its present scope, we
> are holding to a minimum the forces we must commit and tie
> down. . . .
>
> The strategic alternative, enlargement of the war in Korea
> to include Red China, would probably delight the Kremlin
> more than anything else we could do. . . .
>
> Red China is not the powerful nation seeking to dominate

the world. Frankly, in the opinion of the Joint Chiefs of Staff, this strategy would involve us in the wrong war, at the wrong place, at the wrong time, and with the wrong enemy.

After this testimony, the tide began at last to turn against MacArthur. Any impartial observer could see that the Administration had a strong case. One Democratic Senator, Brien McMahon of Connecticut, pointed out to the General that he had not believed in October 1950 that the Chinese Communists would intervene and asked him: "If you happen to be wrong this time and we go into an all-out war, I want to find out how you propose in your mind to defend the American Nation against that war."

"That doesn't happen to be my responsibility, Senator," MacArthur replied. "My responsibilities were in the Pacific, and the Joint Chiefs of Staff and the various agencies of the Government are working day and night for an over-all solution to the global problem. Now I am not familiar with their studies. I haven't gone into it. I have been desperately occupied on the other side of the world, and to discuss in detail things that I haven't even superficially touched doesn't contribute in any way, shape, or manner to the information of this committee or anybody else."

"General," Senator McMahon observed, "I think you make the point very well that I want to make; that the Joint Chiefs and the President of the United States, the Commander in Chief, has to look at this thing on a global basis and a global defense. You as a theater commander by your own statement have not made that kind of study, and yet you advise to push forward with a course of action that may involve us in that global conflict."

To this, the General rejoined: "Everything that is involved in international relationships, Senator, amounts to a gamble, risk. You have to take the risks."

Further risks, however, were exactly what the Administration was not prepared to take. The risk of a third world war with China or Russia or both had been run and apparently avoided, and now President Truman, who did not appear at the hearings, simply wanted to find some way to end the fighting in Korea. Nevertheless, one Republican Senator, Leverett Saltonstall of Massachusetts, wanted to know how the Chinese Communists could have created the present stalemate and how the President, MacArthur, Acheson, and the Joint Chiefs could have so misjudged their early threats to enter the conflict and their ability to do so effectively. Acheson spent eight days on the witness stand, and at one point Saltonstall put the question to him simply and directly: "They really fooled us when it comes right down to it, didn't they?"

There wasn't much that Acheson could reply to this, except to admit with brief and rather refreshing candor: "Yes, sir."

When the hearings ended, MacArthur had gained no new converts and nothing had really changed. In Acheson's opinion, the inquiry "exhausted both committees, bored the press and the public, publicized a considerable amount of classified material, and successfully defused the explosive 'MacArthur issue.'"

On June 23, Jacob Malik, the chief of the Soviet delegation to the United Nations, proposed a cease-fire and the undertaking of negotiations to bring peace to Korea. The United States ascertained that the Russians were acting with the acquiescence of the Chinese, whose armies in Korea had reached the limits of their effectiveness, and directed General Ridgway on June 29 to communicate with the Communist high command for the purpose of arranging truce talks. These talks began on July 10 at Kaesong, a small town one mile south of the 38th Parallel, but the fighting continued.

General MacArthur settled down in the Waldorf Towers and from there went forth on many speaking engagements from Boston to the Alamo in San Antonio. As before, he was greeted everywhere with acclaim. But the acclaim did not turn out to be negotiable into a political endorsement that could change national policy. MacArthur was being cheered as a military hero and as a patriotic symbol. Even his most devoted conservative Republican supporters did not interpret the cheering for the General as a demand from the voters to widen the Korean War.

MacArthur did not seem to realize that his time had passed. He did not appear to understand that the Second World War, of which he was an authentic hero, was the last of the big traditional wars into which nations committed their entire resources. Korea was a watershed moment in which traditional wars gave way to limited ones. The stupendous bombs now in existence had made total wars, and total victories, unthinkable. The American people were more than ready to cheer Mac-Arthur. But they were really not willing to pay the price that would inevitably result from following his recommendations: greater mobilization, higher taxes, and the risk of a big prolonged war with China or Russia or both.

The General did not actively seek the Republican nomination for President in 1952. If he was waiting for a boom to select him, it did not develop. From a realistic political standpoint, both his age, seventy-one, and his fourteen-year absence from the United States made him an unsuitable presidential candidate. MacArthur strongly supported the conservative Republican front-runner, Senator Taft, who made inquiries in early June 1952 to determine if the General would be available as a vice-presidential running mate. MacArthur agreed to Taft's proposal after the Ohio Senator declared that he would give the General a voice in the formulation of foreign policy and deputize him to take responsibility for national security as deputy commander-in-chief of the armed forces.

At the Republican National Convention on the night of July 7, 1952, MacArthur delivered the keynote address. He was accorded an uproarious welcome as he entered the convention hall dressed in civilian clothes for the first time at a public appearance. The General's keynote speech hit hard at the Democratic Administration as he declared that "Foreign policy has been as tragically in error as has domestic policy."

After the speech, however, no delegates placed MacArthur's name in nomination, and it did not go to Senator Taft. Dwight

Eisenhower was nominated on the first ballot. He chose Richard Nixon as his running mate.

MacArthur returned to the Waldorf Towers, which he made his permanent residence, and on August 1, 1952, accepted a long-standing offer from James H. Rand to become Chairman of the Board of Remington Rand, which later merged with the Sperry Corporation to become Sperry Rand. Eisenhower was elected President, partly as a result of the voters' disenchantment with the Democrats over the continuing stalemate in Korea and his campaign promise to go there and attempt to find an honorable end to the fighting.

Upon his return from Korea, the President-elect met with MacArthur on December 17, 1952, to obtain his views on the situation. The meeting was held at the New York City residence of John Foster Dulles. The Secretary of State designate, Eisenhower, and MacArthur were the only people present.

MacArthur presented to them in writing, so that there could be no misunderstanding, a "Memorandum on Ending the Korean War." The lengthy memorandum recommended that the President of the United States hold a two-party conference with Premier Stalin aimed at reaching an agreement on international peace. Among the measures designed to achieve this goal, the United States would "agree to the principle that in Europe all foreign troops should be removed from Germany and Austria, and in Asia from Japan and Korea."

MacArthur went on to recommend "(g) That at such a conference, the Soviet be informed that should an agreement not be reached, it would be our intention to clear North Korea of enemy forces. (This could be accomplished through the atomic bombing of enemy military concentrations and installations in North Korea and the sowing of fields of suitable radio-active materials, the by-product of atomic manufacture, to close major lines of enemy supply and communications leading south from the Yalu, with simultaneous amphibious landings on both coasts of North Korea); "(h) That the Soviet should be further informed that, in such eventuality, it would probably become necessary to neutralize Red China's capability to wage modern war. (This could be accomplished by the destruction of Red China's limited airfields and industrial and supply bases, the cutting off of her tenuous supply lines from the Soviet and the landing of China's Nationalist forces in Manchuria near the mouth of the Yalu, with limited continuing logistical support until such time as the communist government of China has fallen. This concept would become the great bargaining lever to induce the Soviet to agree upon honorable conditions toward international accord. Should all efforts to arrive at a satisfactory agreement fail, then this phase of the plan should be considered in the light of conditions then existing)."

After studying the plan, Dulles commented that it was "a bold and imaginative one and could well succeed. I believe, however, that Eisenhower should first consolidate his position as President before attempting so ambitious and comprehensive a program. It might take him a year to do so." This was, of course, a deferential and diplomatically worded brush-off.

Eisenhower never did follow the advice of his former commander in the Philippines or consult with him after this meeting. As President, he continued Truman's policy of keeping Korea a limited war in an atomic era, avoiding risks that might embroil the United States in an Asiatic land war with China, and seeking an end to the struggle at the conference table. Finally, after many more weary months of fighting and negotiating, an armistice was signed on July 27, 1953. A hush settled over the blasted landscape of a Korea politically divided as it had been on June 25, 1950.

One result of the armistice was the return of 4435 American prisoners of war from Communist captivity. The prisoners were different from those captured in the seven previous major wars in which the United States had fought, for they were the first Americans to have been subjected to intensive political indoctrination. The Defense Department was aware that at least some of the prisoners had fallen victim to this indoctrination. Twenty-one Americans refused repatriation, stating that they preferred to live under communism. Others had made propaganda radio broadcasts for the Chinese, which were monitored by the Defense Department. This kind of behavior was strange, and something new in American history.

The Army, which had supplied about 90 percent of the servicemen who fought in Korea and therefore about the same percentage of captives, conducted an official study of the conduct of the 3973 soldiers who returned home. The study revealed that though the Chinese had failed in their systematic attempt at mass conversion to communism, the "thought reform" effort in the prison camps along the Yalu did produce disquieting results. One out of seven Army prisoners was guilty of serious collaboration. Their disloyal acts included informing on fellow prisoners, writing or broadcasting anti-American propaganda, and agreeing to spy for the enemy when repatriated. And this collaboration had been induced not by "brainwashing" or torture, but by constant mental indoctrination blending leniency with pressure.

In addition to the collaboration with the enemy, there had been a widespread breakdown in morale and discipline in the prison camps. The offenses to traditional military discipline ranged from refusing to obey superior officers to stealing food from weaker comrades to, in the most extreme provable case, the murder of two sick prisoners by another American by throwing them out of a hut into the snow.

Both the collaboration and the breakdown in discipline were the result of complex factors, but also had one basic origin. Most of the captured Americans were seventeen-to-twenty-one-year-old draftees whose formal education had stopped on the average with the ninth grade. Such men knew little about communism or China or the political reasons for their being in North Korea. Certainly they had in no way been prepared for the entry of the Chinese Communists into the war or for the techniques of the skilled indoctrinators who manipulated their minds. The Army had trained them physically, but the old instructions in the training manuals to provide an enemy only with name, rank, birth date, and serial number were simply not adequate for resisting the "thought reform" process. Just as MacArthur and the Administration were surprised by the Chinese entry into the war, the Army was surprised, too, and had not prepared its men for the new techniques they encountered in the Chinese prison camps.

As a result of what happened in the camps, President Eisenhower promulgated on August 17, 1955, a new Code of Conduct for Members of the Armed Forces of the United States. This unprecedented document, whose contents it had never before been thought necessary to formulate, spelled out in simple language how the United States Government expected its servicemen to behave should they be captured in future wars. After Korea, it was obvious that wars would no longer be confined to the battlefield.

MacArthur was never appointed to any office by either of the two Eisenhower Administrations. But the General lived on to make further speeches and to receive further honors. In July, 1961, he undertook what he described as a "sentimental journey" to the Philippines as the invited guest of that nation on the fifteenth anniversary of its independence. In May, 1962, he went to West Point to receive the Sylvanus Thayer Award for distinguished service to the United States. In an emotional extemporaneous address, MacArthur told the assembled Corps of Cadets: "The shadows are lengthening for me. The twilight is here. My days of old have vanished—tone and tint. They have gone glimmering through the dreams of things that were."

President Kennedy invited the General in August 1962 to the White House for an informal three-hour luncheon discussion. On January 26, 1964, MacArthur was honored at the Waldorf on his eighty-fourth birthday. President Johnson sent a telegram calling him "one of the authentic American heroes of this century." But nobody in political or military authority was really listening to the advice of the old soldier, who did gradually fade away.

MacArthur died on April 5, 1964, after a long illness at Walter Reed Medical Center in Washington at the age of eighty-four. His body was flown to New York City to lie in state, as he had requested, in the Seventh Regiment Armory on Park Avenue. In one day, thirty-five thousand mourners, at the rate of three thousand an hour, passed by the open casket. Then the plain steel Army casket was sent by train to Washington, where it was displayed in the Capitol Rotunda. President Johnson, seemingly on the verge of crying, placed a wreath at the open casket's head.

Former President Eisenhower did not appear at the Capitol Rotunda. He was on vacation in California with his wife. Eisenhower announced that she did not fly and that he did not want to appear without her. Former President Truman did not attend the ceremonies, either. After they ended, MacArthur's body was flown to its final resting place in Norfolk, Virginia. This was the birthplace of his mother, and she was to have returned to her hometown for Douglas's birth in 1880. Instead, she was delayed, and he was born at an Army post in Arkansas. Now the Norfolk city fathers had converted their classic one-hundred-fourteen-year-old courthouse and designated it the MacArthur Memorial. In the presence of family and friends, the General's casket was placed in a crypt beneath the rotunda. Then the tomb was sealed, ending a military career that was not likely to be repeated in America. A bugler sounded taps, whose mournful notes echoed inside the walls of the rotunda. The walls were inscribed with some of the General's more famous quotations, a list of his achievements, and the names of the campaigns he had won. There was no inscription for the drive to the Yalu River.

Epilogue

Seven months after the General's death, a filmed television series entitled "The Conflicts of Harry S. Truman" was shown throughout the United States. Much of the commentary accompanying the film was supplied by the eighty-year-old, but still peppery, former President himself. In one of the segments, filmed before MacArthur's death, Truman gave his version of why he had relieved the General thirteen years before:

> MacArthur made the suggestion that we cross the Yalu River and that we bomb troops over in Manchuria. But he was not allowed to do it. We were almost in a war with China and Russia . . . and what we were afraid of was if we went up and made all-out war in North Korea, immediately, the Russians would come in and they would not only do that, they would overrun that part of Europe that was already free. . . .
>
> Time after time, MacArthur went his own way in national policies. And he didn't seem to care whether he upset the national policy of the Government of the United States or not. . . . He was trying to get himself in good with one of the big parties of the Government . . . so that he could be President of the United States. He didn't fool anybody—and least of all did he fool me!

There was a statement that MacArthur stirred things up so that he would be the leader of the disgruntled people who were against what was being done there. Well, I was satisfied that was the case. And it was the last thing in the world that a commanding general of a republic has any right to do.

Cabell Phillips, author of *The Truman Presidency,* once asked the former President during an interview if he agreed with many of his admirers who felt that his relief of MacArthur was the single most courageous act of his Presidency.

"Courage didn't have anything to do with it," Truman snapped. "General MacArthur was insubordinate and I fired him. That's all there was to it."

But, of course, there was more to it than that. Truman won his struggle with MacArthur, and the supremacy of the civilian branch of the government over the military was once more firmly asserted. It was fortunate that Truman did prevail. The benefit of the hindsight of the American experience in Vietnam is now available. It is not difficult to understand that following MacArthur's recommendations on the largest Asiatic country would have resulted in the making of a quagmire much worse than the one caused by the Vietnam intervention.

Truman's foreign policies remained the basis for those of succeeding administrations, both Republican and Democratic. Korea was not united, but the aggression of the North Korean Communists was repulsed. This was perhaps a poor substitute for victory, but it was an acceptable substitute for global war or a prolonged Asian land war. However, because of the un-popularity of the Korean War, President Truman remained too weak at home politically to bring it to an end. The hope offered by Dwight Eisenhower that he could end it satisfactorily con-tributed to his victory over Adlai Stevenson in the 1952 Presi-dential election. And Eisenhower, a Republican and a vic-torious general who was not vulnerable to charges of being an appeaser, did negotiate an armistice with the North Korean and Chinese Communists that accepted the division of Korea and peace without victory.

From this stalemate the new Communist government of

China nevertheless emerged as a world power. Grudging admiration was accorded by the newly emerging and nonaligned Asian and African countries for the way that the Chinese armies had surprised the mighty Western forces of the United Nations and fought them to a standstill. The outcome of the war enabled the Communist Party to deepen, expand, and consolidate its position as the legitimate ruler of mainland China.

But for more than two decades after 1950, the Chinese Year of the Tiger, a Government that had ruled since then one-fourth of the world's people remained without a seat in the United Nations and without diplomatic recognition by the United States. It was not until July 15, 1971, when President Nixon announced that he would visit China at the invitation of Premier Chou En-lai to "seek the normalization of relations between the two countries," that the reestablishment of communications at last appeared possible. This was a bold and historic move by President Nixon, who as a Senator had once led the political clamor of the China lobby to ostracize Peking from the community of "peace-loving" nations. It was a major step toward thawing relations that were frozen by the miscalculations and misunderstandings of the United Nations drive to the Yalu and Chinese intervention in the Korean War.

With the passage of time, the motivation for Chinese intervention does not seem as clear-cut as it did at the height of the Cold War, nor does the branding of China as an aggressor by the United Nations appear altogether justified. A good case could be made for Peking acting out of Chinese national interest, rather than as the dutiful puppet of Moscow in a monolithic Communist plan to attack and enslave the free world. Although the Peking archives are not likely to be opened for Western inspection, it is entirely likely that the Chinese would not have come into the war if MacArthur's forces had remained at the 38th Parallel in the fall of 1950 and not driven on to the Yalu. From the Chinese point of view, which is as valid for them as ours is for us, the Chinese Communist leaders may have been reacting to deep-rooted fears posed by the advance of foreign armies up the traditional Korean invasion corridor bordering Manchuria.

That the Chinese were not puppets of Moscow and that they were prepared to fight all comers over threats to their borders was underscored with the passage of time. Until around 1958, China accepted enormous benefits in loans and technical aid from her Russian allies. Soviet technicians helped launch China as a nuclear power with a reactor set up near Peking in 1958. But then, as the policies of Mao Tse-tung became more nationalistic and China attempted instant industrialization on its own through the Great Leap Forward, the Sino-Soviet alliance began to crack. The split widened into harsh polemics in the early 1960's as China sought to go it alone and capture the ideological leadership of the Communist world revolution. The split became so wide that the 24th Congress of the Soviet Communist Party held in April 1971 named the United States and China as its two main rivals in the world.

The 4500-mile border between China and Russia, fought over by both nations since 1685, meanwhile became a line of bitter contention once more. The frontier falls naturally into two major sectors—the Central Asian and the Manchurian, with the nominally independent country of Mongolia in between. In March 1969, Soviet and Chinese troops engaged in limited warfare along the frontier in the Ussuri River area of Manchuria. By the summer of 1971, both nations had military forces of around two million men on either side of the disputed 4500-mile-long border. But a major war over the border has not broken out. Perhaps the Soviet and the Chinese Communist leaders realize that one nuclear power cannot win an old-fashioned victory over another nuclear power and that to try would be infeasible or, in the phrase of Confucius, like "climbing a tree to catch a fish."

In Korea, there was no real peace along the border between the north and south more than two decades after the fighting began there. Just as none of the combatants ever officially declared war, a formal peace agreement was never reached. The armistice signed on July 27, 1953, simply led to one of the longest truces in history and the establishment of a demilitarized zone. This no-man's-land severs Korea for one hundred and fifty miles from sea to sea and is two and one-half miles wide. Right in the middle of it, at Panmunjom, uniformed members of the Military Armistice Commission meet irregularly to hear specific complaints about breaches in the armistice agreement. There is much exchange of invective at these meetings, though this is undoubtedly better than an exchange of bullets.

The truce continues in a state of suspended animation with a strange life of its own. Along the stationary front-line runs an element of tension and an atmosphere of bristling hostility. Small but bloody encounters occasionally erupt. Bands of North Korean infiltrators are caught tunneling under the meshed barbed wire and executed by South Koreans. A sniper fires a rifle shot in the darkness and a soldier dies. These minor fights could erupt into a major clash at any time. But China has displayed no interest in instigating an attack by her North Korean allies.

American, as well as South Korean, soldiers keep watch along the demilitarized zone. The young Americans patrol valleys and ridge lines once permeated with the stench of death and whose old names some of them may remember—Alligator Ridge, T-Bone Ridge, Pork Chop Hill. The American soldiers are reminders that the Korean War never really ended. It was just forgotten as the attention of the United States was concentrated upon a new Asian land war. This, too, was a major undeclared war into which the United States was taken by presidential decision and without the formal consent of Congress, although this time the United Nations did not sanction American intervention. In Vietnam, successive American Presidents relied heavily for guidance upon the intelligence community, and the expert counsel of a small group of civilian crisis managers and experienced military men.

In dealing with South Vietnam, American policy-makers may have been encouraged by the relatively successful outcome

of the intervention in Korea. There, the United States was able
to stabilize the southern half of an Asiatic country, leave most
of its defense to the natives, and provide economic assistance
that resulted in a marked increase in living standards. But the
analogy was a deceptive one. The war in Vietnam proved
much more difficult, and the Vietnamese a different kind of
people.

However, the most hawkish of presidential advisers never
urged the invasion of North Vietnam by American ground
forces or the invasion of North Vietnam by South Vietnamese
ground troops backed by American air power. North Vietnam
lies on China's doorstep, and the possibility of Chinese intervention was always present. This possibility was underscored
in March 1971, when Premier Chou En-lai visited Hanoi and
announced that China and North Vietnam were as closely
linked as "lips and teeth." A joint communiqué signed by Chou
and Hanoi's Premier Pham Van Dong declared that the Chinese people would "take all necessary measures, not flinching
even from the greatest national sacrifices" to aid the North
Vietnamese if the United States should "go down the road of
expanding its war of aggression."

This time, the United States Government took the warnings
of Chou En-lai seriously and appeared to have learned at
least one lesson from the miscalculations of the Year of the
Tiger. But it was not until October 25, 1971, that Peking's
policies could be expressed officially in the United Nations. On
that date mainland China's long isolation from the international community came to an end when the General Assembly
voted by a decisive margin to expel the Chinese Nationalist
Government and to admit the Peking regime it had once
branded as an aggressor for its intervention in Korea.

The vote took place after a tense meeting lasting more than
eight hours. When the roll call was finished at 9:47 P.M.,
Salim Ahmed Salim, Tanzania's chief delegate, danced vic-
toriously in the front row of the General Assembly Hall.
George Bush, the American chief delegate, remained slumped
in his seat. While the United States had finally reversed its

militant policy of keeping mainland China out of the U.N., it had lost its fight against the expulsion of the Chinese Nationalists. Hardly anyone noted that the historic vote took place exactly twenty-one years after Chinese Communist troops had first attacked U.N. forces at Onjong in North Korea.

The U.N. vote did represent a defeat for the United States, but it was not fatal in view of President Nixon's dramatic change of American policy from hostility to a search for accommodation with the Chinese Communists. On November 30, 1971, the White House announced that beginning on February 21, 1972, President Nixon would visit three Chinese cities, Hangchow, Shanghai, and Peking, and hold discussions with Chou En-lai and Chairman Mao Tse-tung.

Henry Kissinger, Nixon's adviser on national security affairs, explained one of the reasons for the President's unique journey. It was in the interest of both China and the United States, he said, "that we understand what we are about and that on those matters that are in our common interest we know how to cooperate." The President hoped that the establishment of a system of communicating opposing views would result in avoiding in the future "very dramatic, set-piece encounters" with the Chinese.

Sources

Much has been written, of course, about the Korean War. An unprecedented amount of information was made available as a result of the MacArthur hearings in 1951. Since that time, MacArthur, Whitney, Acheson, Truman, Collins, and Ridgway have all published volumes giving their versions of the events described in this book, and more information has come to light on Chinese Communist motivations and actions. What I have attempted to do is to distill all of these sources into a meaningful narrative. The bibliography that follows is not meant to be exhaustive, but lists only those works which I found to be of specific use.

SELECTED BIBLIOGRAPHY

OFFICIAL DOCUMENTS

UNITED STATES

Military Situation in the Far East. Hearings before the Armed
  Services Committee and Foreign Relations Committee, United

States Senate, 82nd Congress, 1st Session. Washington: Government Printing Office, 1951. These five volumes consist of testimony taken during the MacArthur hearings, which ran for forty-three days. Some 1,239,750 words of testimony taken were deleted from the printed public record by the official censor, Admiral Arthur C. Davis, for security reasons. However, the five volumes contain as complete a record of the basic issues and strategic policies of the period of the Korean War covered in this book as is likely to be made available to the public.

Substance of Statements made at Wake Island Conference on October 15, 1950, compiled from notes kept by the conferees from Washington (compilation by General Bradley). Washington: Government Printing Office, 1951.

Appleman, Roy E.: *South to the Naktong, North to the Yalu June-November 1950*. Washington, D.C.: Office of the Chief of Military History, Department of the Army, 1961. This is Volume 1 of the comprehensive official U.S. Army military history, *The United States Army in the Korean War*.

Montross, Lynn and Nicholas A. Canzona: *U.S. Marine Operations in Korea, 1950-1953*. Vol. 3. Washington, D.C.: Headquarters, U.S. Marine Corps, 1957. A detailed description of Marine Corps military activities in Korea in the fall of 1950 and the winter of 1951 is given in this volume.

GREAT BRITAIN

Parliament. *Debates. House of Commons.*

UNITED NATIONS

Official Records of the General Assembly.
Official Records of the Security Council.

NEWSPAPERS AND PERIODICALS

Chicago *Tribune,* Los Angeles *Times,* New York *Herald Tribune, The New York Times,* Washington *Post, The Times* (London), *Life, Time, Newsweek, U.S. News & World Report.*

BOOKS, ARTICLES, PERIODICALS

Acheson, Dean: *Present at the Creation*. New York, 1969.
Barclay, C. N.: *The First Commonwealth Division, The Story of*

British Commonwealth Land Forces in Korea, 1950-1953. Aldershot (England), 1954.

Blumenson, Martin: "Task Force Kingston." *Army* magazine, April 1964.

Burns, James M.: *Roosevelt: The Soldier of Freedom.* New York, 1970.

Carlson, Evans: *Two Stars of China.* New York, 1940.

Catledge, Turner: *My Life and The Times.* New York, 1971.

Ch'en, Jerome: *Mao Papers.* New York, 1970.

Collins, J. Lawton: *War in Peacetime.* Boston, 1969.

Eisenhower, Dwight: *The White House Years—Mandate for Change.* New York, 1963.

Fairbank, John K.: *The United States and China.* 3rd ed. Cambridge, Mass., 1971.

Feis, Herbert: *China Tangle.* Princeton, N.J., 1953.

Futrell, Robert F.: *The United States Air Force in Korea, 1950-1953.* New York, 1961.

George, Alexander L.: *The Chinese Communist Army in Action.* New York, 1967.

Griffith, Samuel B.: *The Chinese People's Liberation Army.* New York, 1967.

Gugeler, Russell A.: *Combat Actions in Korea.* Washington, 1954.

Gunther, John: *The Riddle of MacArthur.* New York, 1951.

Heinl, Robert: *Victory at High Tide—The Inchon-Seoul Campaign.* New York, 1968.

Hersey, John: *Men on Bataan.* New York, 1943.

Higgins, Trumbull: *Korea and the Fall of MacArthur.* New York, 1960.

Hsü, Immanuel C. Y.: *The Rise of Modern China.* New York, 1970.

James, Dorris Clayton: *The Years of MacArthur. Volume 1. 1880-1941.* Boston, 1971.

Kenney, George C.: *The MacArthur I Knew.* New York, 1951.

Kinkead, Eugene: *In Every War But One.* New York, 1959.

Leckie, Robert: *Conflict.* New York, 1962.

Lichterman, Martin: *To the Yalu and Back.* Inter-University Case Program #92. Indianapolis, 1963.

Long, Gavin: *MacArthur As Military Commander.* Princeton, N.J., 1969.

MacArthur, Douglas: *Reminiscences.* New York, 1964.

McLellan, David S.: "Dean Acheson and the Korean War." *Political Science Quarterly,* Vol. LXXXIII, No. 1, March 1968.

Magruder, John: "The Chinese as a Fighting Man." *Foreign Affairs,* Vol. 9, No. 3, April 1931.

Marshall, S. L. A.: *The River and the Gauntlet.* New York, 1953.

Neustadt, Richard: *Presidential Power.* New York, 1960.

Panikkar, K. M.: *In Two Chinas.* London, 1955.

Phillips, Cabell: *The Truman Presidency.* New York, 1966.

Pogue, Forrest C., with the editorial assistance of Gordon Harrison: *George C. Marshall: Education of a General 1880-1939.* New York, 1963.

————: *George C. Marshall: Ordeal and Hope 1939-1942.* New York, 1966.

Rankin, Karl Lott: *China Assignment.* Seattle, 1964.

Rees, David: *Korea: The Limited War.* New York, 1964.

Ridgway, Matthew B.: *Soldier.* New York, 1956.

————: *The Korean War,* New York, 1967.

Rigg, Robert B.: *Red China's Fighting Hordes.* Harrisburg, Pa., 1951.

Rommel, Erwin: *The Rommel Papers.* B. H. Liddell-Hart, ed. New York, 1953.

Rovere, Richard H. and Arthur M. Schlesinger, Jr.: *The General and the President.* New York, 1951.

Ryan, Cornelius and Frank Kelley: *MacArthur: Man of Action.* New York, 1950.

Salisbury, Harrison E.: *War Between China and Russia.* New York, 1969.

Sebald, W. J.: *With MacArthur in Japan: A Personal History of the Occupation.* New York, 1965.

Spanier, John W.: *The Truman-MacArthur Controversy and the Korean War.* Cambridge, Mass., 1959.

Steinberg, Alfred: *The Man from Missouri: The Life and Times of Harry S. Truman.* New York, 1962.

Styron, William: *The Way of the Warrior.* New York, 1971.

Tuchman, Barbara: *Stilwell and the American Experience in China, 1911-1945.* New York, 1971.

Tugwell, Rexford G.: *The Democratic Roosevelt.* New York, 1957.

Truman, Harry S.: *Years of Trial and Hope,* Vol. 2.: *Memoirs.* New York, 1956.

Westover, John G.: *Combat Support in Korea.* Washington, 1955.

White, William Lindsay: *The Captives of Korea.* New York, 1957.

White, William S.: *The Taft Story.* New York, 1954.

Whiting, Allen S.: *China Crosses the Yalu: The Decision to Enter the Korean War*. New York, 1960.

Whitney, Courtney: *MacArthur: His Rendezvous with History*. New York, 1956.

Williams, T. Harry: *Huey Long*. New York, 1969.

Willoughby, Charles A. and John Chamberlain: *MacArthur 1941-1951*. New York, 1954.

CHAPTER NOTES

ONE:

The physical description of the Wake Island meeting is taken from contemporary accounts in *The New York Times* and *Time* magazine. The personal reactions of Whitney, MacArthur, and Truman are drawn from their books listed in the bibliography. The quotation by Turner Catledge is from his listed book. Other sources were Panikkar's *In Two Chinas;* State Department Bulletin XXIII; and the *Official Records of the General Assembly* of the U.N. Miss Anderson's stenographic notes of the conference are published in full in *Substance of Statements* listed in the bibliography.

TWO:

Based on the listed books by Truman, MacArthur, Panikkar, Rovere and Schlesinger and reports in *The New York Times* and *Time.*

THREE:

Drawn from the listed books by MacArthur, Gunther, Kenney, Ryan and Kelley, Whitney, James, Hersey, Steinberg, Tugwell, Williams, Heinl, Sebald, Willoughby, Acheson, Pogue, and the study in *Political Science Quarterly* by McLellan. The comment about Whitney by Bowers is taken from Bowers's article "How Japan Won the War" in *The New York Times Magazine,* August 30, 1970.

FOUR:

Based on books by Griffith, George, Tuchman, Rigg, Panikkar, Ch'en, Hsü, and S. L. A. Marshall.

FIVE:

Drawn from Ridgway's *The Korean War,* Collins's *War in Peacetime,* and the listed books by Appleman and Willoughby in addition to reports in *The New York Times* and *Time.*

SIX:

From Appleman, Barclay, Futrell, Griffith, S. L. A. Marshall, the official Marine Corps history by Montross and Canzona, and *Time*.

SEVEN:

From Acheson, MacArthur, Burns, Phillips, Steinberg, Truman, Montross and Canzona, *The New York Times* and *Time*.

EIGHT:

Fairbank, Whiting, George, Griffith, Willoughby, Rankin, Ridgway, Appleman, *The New York Times*.

NINE:

Derived from the listed books by Appleman, Montross and Canzona, Acheson, Leckie, Neustadt, Ridgway, Truman, Phillips, MacArthur, Whitney, Rommel, and reports in the New York *Herald Tribune* and *The New York Times*.

TEN:

From the books by Griffith, S. L. A. Marshall, George, MacArthur, Collins, Ridgway, William Lindsay White, Kinkead, Willoughby, Whitney, Truman, and Appleman. The story of "Task Force Kingston" is condensed from the article of that name by Captain Martin Blumenson, which appeared in *Army* magazine, April 1964.

ELEVEN:

The story of Colonel Faith and his command was taken from Russell A. Gugeler's *Combat Actions in Korea,* an interesting study of several small unit actions. Other sources for this chapter were the listed books by Westover, Acheson, Montross and Canzona, Appleman, Collins, and reports in *Time* and *Newsweek*.

TWELVE:

In writing this chapter, I drew upon reports in *The New York Times,* New York *Herald Tribune,* Chicago *Tribune, Time, Life,* and the listed books by MacArthur, Truman, Acheson, and Ridgway.

THIRTEEN:

Based on the listed books by Ridgway, MacArthur, Collins, and Truman.

FOURTEEN:

This chapter is based on the official records of the U.N. General Assembly and Security Council, the listed books by Truman, MacArthur, and Acheson, and reports in *Time* and *The New York Times*.

FIFTEEN:

For this chapter I drew upon the listed books by Acheson, MacArthur, William S. White, William Lindsay White, Whitney, Eisenhower, Kinkead, Styron, *Military Situation in the Far East,* and reports in *The New York Times,* New York *Herald Tribune,* Chicago *Tribune,* Los Angeles *Times,* Washington *Post,* and *The Times* (London).

EPILOGUE:

Truman's television comments are printed in *U.S. News & World Report* of November 30, 1964. I have also drawn on the listed book by Phillips and reports in *The New York Times.*

INDEX

Account of the War in Africa
(Rommel), 105
Acheson, Dean, 11, 33, 34, 68,
69, 73, 74, 77, 79, 83, 85,
96, 97, 98–99, 100, 111, 117,
119, 120, 121, 140–41, 142,
145, 146–47, 151, 152, 159,
164, 172, 175, 176, 179, 181,
185, 191, 194, 197
background of, 99
Alanbrooke, Field Marshal, 2
Almond, Edward, 31, 49, 50, 52–
53, 64, 66, 93, 94, 109, 120,
124–26, 127, 130–31
Anderson, Clarence, 58
Anderson, Vernice, 5, 7
Antung, Manchuria, 74
Armentrout, Robert Lee, 124
Art of War (Sun Tzu), 46
Atom bomb, 86–87, 117–18, 130,
141, 146
Attlee, Clement, 117, 118, 129,
147
 conference with Truman, 140,
141, 142
Austin, Warren, 141, 144

Baillie, Hugh, 118, 169
Baker, Newton, 19
Balboni, Joseph, 61
Bao Dai, 143, 144
Barkley, Alben, 110
Barr, David, 45, 93, 94
"Bataan Gang," 32
Bender, George, 180

Berlin airlift, 70
Bigart, Homer, 106
Bonus Marchers, 22–24
Bowers, Faubion, 31
Bradley, Omar, 5, 35, 50, 75, 78,
97, 151, 162, 175, 176, 195
Brady, "Diamond Jim," 18
Brooks, Louise Cromwell, *see*
MacArthur, Louise
Brooks, Walter, 21
Bunker, Laurence, 5
Bush, George, 209

Campbell, James, 127, 129
Carlson, Evans, 45
Cates, Clifton, 94
Catledge, Turner, 3
Central Intelligence Agency, 11,
31, 101
Chiang Kai-shek, 39, 44–45, 70,
72, 83, 86, 90, 99, 138–39,
140, 161, 164, 165, 167
Chinese People's Committee in
Defense of World Peace and
Against American Aggression,
81
Chosan, North Korea, 51
Chosin Reservoir, 53, 63, 64,
116, 122, 123, 124, 126, 131
Chou En-lai, 5–6, 10, 11, 39,
82–83, 100, 148, 206, 209,
210
Chu Teh, 83
Church, John, 102
Churchill, Winston, 2, 117–18

221